A REPENTANT HEART

The Joy of Restoring Intimacy
with God

Dudley J. Delffs

NAVPRESS

BRINGING TRUTH TO LIFE
NavPress Publishing Group
P.O. Box 35001, Colorado Springs, Colorado 80935

The Navigators is an international Christian organization. Jesus Christ gave His followers the Great Commission to go and make disciples (Matthew 28:19). The aim of The Navigators is to help fulfill that commission by multiplying laborers for Christ in every nation.

NavPress is the publishing ministry of The Navigators. NavPress publications are tools to help Christians grow. Although publications alone cannot make disciples or change lives, they can help believers learn biblical discipleship, and apply what they learn to their lives and ministries.

© 1995 by Dudley J. Delffs

Library of Congress Catalog Card Number:
    94-43458
ISBN 08910-98771

Some of the anecdotal illustrations in this book are true to life and are included with the permission of the persons involved. All other illustrations are composites of real situations, and any resemblance to people living or dead is coincidental.

Unless otherwise identified, all Scripture quotations in this publication are taken from the *New American Standard Bible* (NASB), © The Lockman Foundation 1960, 1962, 1963, 1968, 1971, 1972, 1973, 1975, 1977. Other versions used include: the *HOLY BIBLE: NEW INTERNATIONAL VERSION* ® (NIV®). Copyright ©1973, 1978, 1984 by International Bible Society. Used by permission of Zondervan Publishing House, all rights reserved; the *New King James Version* (NKJV), copyright © 1979, 1980, 1982, 1990, Thomas Nelson Inc., Publishers; and *The Message* by Eugene H. Peterson, copyright ©1993, used by permission of NavPress Publishing Group.

Delffs, Dudley J.
    A repentant heart : the joy of restoring intimacy with God / by Dudley J. Delffs.
        p.   cm.
    Includes bibliographical references.
    ISBN 0-89109-877-1
    1. Repentance—Christianity. 2. Change—religious aspects—Christianity. 3. God—Worship and love. I. Title.
BT800.D44   1995
234'.5—dc20   94-43458
                                                                   CIP

Printed in the United States of America

1 2 3 4 5 6 7 8 9 10/99 98 97 97 96 95

CONTENTS

—

Introduction

DO YOU WANT
TO CHANGE?

—

D o you want to change? Do you struggle? Do you wonder what real repentance looks like in your life?
Chances are, if you've picked up this book, the answer
to those questions is yes. My personal answer is yes as well.

But I have a confession to make: I began this book halfheartedly. While I planned in earnest to chronicle my own life-
struggles toward God as well as my experiences as a counselor,
I realized immediately that I had begun a project that required
more than just my ideas and insights. It required my heart. This
seems obvious after the fact, but it took me quite by surprise at
the time. Although I knew I wasn't going to be offering a one-
two-three formula for repentance, I foolishly hoped I could distance myself from the material under the pretense of organizing
my chapters.

Fortunately, I discovered before the book was even half
finished that something was terribly wrong inside me. I couldn't
just plop down in my office and crank out chapter after chapter,
filling in theological definitions with isolated Bible verses and an
example or two. The essence of repentance, the essence of the

gospel, sparks and requires our heart's greatest attention. It speaks to the fundamental questions of who we are and how we should live. And it speaks to our questions about the God we claim to serve: Who is He, really? Is He good? Where is He in the midst of my deepest struggles? Why doesn't He alleviate my pain?

When I was a boy my family would drive twelve hours to arrive at our Florida vacation site. Like most children, I suffered the tedium of the trip with anxious impatience: "When will we get there? How much farther?" And this was before we even got on the interstate. After an hour or two of playing car games and hearing another estimated arrival time, I would try to sleep. After all, time flies when you sleep, right? "Wake me up when we get there," I'd tell my mom. She would nod and smile knowingly, sure that I'd awaken before we arrived.

I think Christians often approach their lives the same way. Rather than experiencing the wonder, sorrow, and longing of their journeys with God, they reduce life to a safe, manageable stroll along a clearly lit path. Since as Christians we know God is good and that we'll be with Him in Heaven someday, we don't have to feel the full weight of this messy life. We can numb ourselves to painful reality; we can "sleepwalk" through life, with a wake-me-up-when-we-get-there view of Heaven.

Unfortunately, we often do this in "spiritual ways" by memorizing a verse or reducing prayer to a detached monologue. We create formulas to control our lives, spend time in Scripture out of obligation and not passion, seek counseling to eliminate our problems, and read theology to understand God. We end up not wanting to know and love and serve God for who He is, but rather wanting Him to help us get through this life as comfortably as possible. Our thinking goes something like this: Since He's good and He can take away life's hardships, then He should.

Repentance, then, becomes a word to throw out at an old-fashioned revival, a historical term describing our way-back-when salvation decision. However, this perspective is sadly, tragically skewed to point back to ourselves rather than God. *Our plans* are not the purpose of God's existence; His plans are the purpose of ours. Therefore, repentance is an ongoing process, the living out of seeking God and His ways rather than ourselves. A repentant heart seeks to lose itself in knowing God, rather than to find itself in gratifying absorption. "For whoever wishes to save his life shall lose it; but whoever loses his life for My sake shall find it" (Matthew 16:25). The paradox of faith is that we can know who we truly are only by caring more about knowing who God is.

Consequently, we often feel stuck. We know deep down that our walk with God is lacking. We're afraid to feel, afraid to ask hard questions, afraid to wrestle, afraid to trust. We become paralyzed in the tension of knowing Christ has given us new life and still feeling the strong pull of the old here-and-now life. We long for change, for real life-changing pursuit of God. We are desperately thirsty, our souls parched, and we know it.

I believe God continues to quench our thirst with His living water. I believe the call to repentance resonates in our hearts with new meaning, with simplicity and clarity. We yearn to change. We want to go home. Life feels unbearable and we want so much more, someone to trust in who is bigger and better than we are. Someone who cares for us beyond our experience and imagination. We burn to know our Abba Father.

I believe if we're honest, we would all admit to an ongoing struggle with God, with faith, with trusting Him. We are realizing more and more that God will not be managed and reduced to neat theological categories. He intrudes in our lives and penetrates our deepest parts with His mysterious presence. He calls us to repent, to turn from ourselves and toward Him, every day of our lives.

On the wall above my desk where I write is taped my favorite postcard. It is a black-and-white photograph, taken by a Frenchman named Jean-Gilles Quenum—so I'm informed on the back—entitled *Ombre Indiquant La Lumière,* "Shadow Pointing to the Light." A rectangular shot of dusty ground pocked with a few stones and a leaf or two, the picture is divided roughly in horizontal halves by a triangle of shade melting into sunlight. From the darker half, the shadow of a shoulder and arm emerge point-ing at the unseen light source. The outline is graceful and delib-erate, one finger extended like Michelangelo's Adam on the ceiling of the Sistine Chapel in his stretch toward God.

It is a favorite image because it so beautifully and succinctly captures so much of my journey with the Lord. It reminds me of C. S. Lewis's description of this world being the Shadow-lands, the mere shadows of the ultimate spiritual realities of Heaven, the foggy ruins of our fallen world from which we occa-sionally glimpse the glorious beauty and grace of Christ. It reminds me of what I desire in my life, to point at the Light—my Father, His Son, the Spirit—and not at myself. Finally, I am reminded that I am on a journey, a walk of faith in progress even as I write this. The path is often dark and shadowy, and I'm often straying off to some dead-end rabbit trail or stopping to whine about how tired I am or how tight my shoes are. When moments of light shine through with brilliance and clarity, I'm often quick to take credit for them and demand that the entire journey should be just this way—bright, sunny, and carefree. Of course, thank-fully, it is not.

This book is about being a shadow and pointing to the Light. It is about repentance, the process of turning toward God in the midst of every circumstance of our lives. Since repentance as discussed here is not a formula, not three easy steps to that sunny and carefree life, I want to be clear from the start. This is a book about spiritual exploration, some personal and some conceptual, some philosophic and mostly theological, that examines vari-ous barriers to the process of repentance—temptation, addic-tions, pride, self-absorption—and various enablers to repen-tance—sorrow over sinfulness, honesty, integrity, and a passion to love and know our Abba Father through His Son, Jesus Christ.

I am not a professional theologian, but one as all of us are called to be: a living believer struggling and glimpsing God, and seeing my theology grow out of that. I have degrees in litera-ture, creative writing, and Christian counseling. I have coun-seled a little, taught English a lot, and written a novel. I tell you these things by way of introduction, since I believe it's impossible for me to write on this topic without disclosing some of who I am, what I struggle with, and what I believe. I hope you can share my thoughts without necessarily having to agree with them all.

But I certainly don't want this book to be about me. I want it to be relevant and accessible to both new believers as well as more mature saints, to provoke your thinking and spark your heart toward what it means to live a repentant life, to seek God above all else, to remain diligently on His path through a lifetime of change. I want it to better point you to the Light, from one shadow to another, and strengthen your own desire and ability to point others to the same Light.

I pray that you can't read this book halfheartedly, that you're forced to long for God's Light and point to it out of a deep soul-longing. If you're picking up this book in order to overcome a particular vice or uncomfortable habit while keeping the rest of your life largely intact, you will likely be disappointed. This book does not offer steps to overcoming specific problems of behavior, although it does address the most specific problem of all, our inherent selfishness, our neediness of the Father's love, grace, and mercy. Yes, you may see some old habits slipping away, but I pray that you become aware of a much deeper work, a much more thorough and complete change, transforming you. C. S. Lewis describes the process this way:

> When I was a child I often had [a] toothache, and I knew that if I went to my mother she would give me something which would deaden the pain for that night and let me get to sleep. But I did not go to mother—at least, not till the pain became very bad. And the reason I did not go was this. I did not doubt she would give me the aspirin; but I knew that she would also do something else. I knew she would take me to the dentist the next morning. I could not get what I wanted out of her without getting something more, which I did not want. I

wanted immediate relief from pain: but I could not get it
without having my teeth set permanently right. And I
knew those dentists; I knew they started fiddling about
with all sorts of other teeth which had not yet begun to
ache. They would not let sleeping dogs lie; if you gave
them an inch, they took an ell.

Now, if I may put it that way, our Lord is like the
dentist. If you give Him an inch, He will take an ell.
Dozens of people go to Him to be cured of some particular sin which they are ashamed of (like lust or physical
cowardice) or which is obviously spoiling daily life (like
bad temper or drunkenness). Well, He will cure it all
right: but He will not stop there. That may be all you
asked; but if you once call Him in, He will give you the
full treatment.

That is why He warned people to "count the cost"
before becoming Christians. "Make no mistake," He
says, "if you let Me, I will make you perfect. The
moment you put yourself in My hands, that is what you
are in for. Nothing less, or other, than that. You have free
will, and if you choose, you can push Me away. But if
you do not push Me away, understand that I am going to
see this job through."[1]

My prayer is that this book accurately depicts this "full treatment" by exploring what it means to want to change, to have a
repentant heart, to experience the joyful intimacy with our Abba
Father that we so long for. I pray that this book would be a catalyst, to whatever degree, that makes you hungrier for God, wea-
rier of your selfishness and this fallen world in which we live,
more willing to suffer now for the ultimate embrace of the Father
we shall one day have in Heaven.

Do you want to change? Better yet, do you want to know
your Father?

Do not remember the former things,
Nor consider the things of old.
Behold, I will do a new thing,
Now it shall spring forth;
Shall you not know it?
I will even make a road in the wilderness
And rivers in the desert.
—ISAIAH 43:18-19, NKJV

To repent is to come to your senses.
It is not so much something you do as something
that happens. True repentance spends less time
looking at the past and saying,
"I'm sorry," than to the future and saying "Wow!"
—FREDERICK BUECHNER, *Wishful Thinking*

Batter my heart, three-personed God; for You
As yet but knock, breathe, shine, and seek to mend;
That I may rise and stand, o'erthrow me, and bend
Your force to break, blow, burn and make me new.
I, like an usurped town, to another due,
Labor to admit You, but Oh, to no end;
Reason, Your viceroy in me, me should defend,
But is captived, and proves weak and untrue.
Yet dearly I love You, and would be loved fain,
But am betrothed unto Your enemy.
Divorce me, untie or break that knot again;
Take me to You, imprison me, for I,
Except You enthrall me, never shall be free,
Nor ever chaste, except You ravish me.
—JOHN DONNE, *Holy Sonnets*

Jesus began to preach and say,
"Repent, for the kingdom of heaven is at hand."
—MATTHEW 4:17

I

WHY DO I DO WHAT I DON'T WANT TO DO?

S teve was tired of slaving fifty hours a week while his wife Anne didn't seem to appreciate how hard he worked. When he wasn't at the office she expected him to be fixing up around the house, watching the kids, or going to church. It seemed they were always arguing about something. Last night it was her latest shopping spree, way over budget. It wasn't even about money, he thought, but more about his leadership. She was always testing him, pushing him to the limit, demanding more. "I love my wife," Steve said to himself, "I really do. But how can I love a woman who doesn't respect me?"

Now he found himself on his lunch break turning into a familiar parking lot. So what if he looked at certain magazines from time to time? Didn't he deserve some kind of break? A little fantasy never hurt anybody, right? But in the back of his mind, Steve knew he hated his reliance on pornography. He longed to break free and be a better man, but he wasn't sure how.

What would it mean for Steve to repent? He knew pornography deadened and drained his heart toward his wife. He knew his fantasy life only compounded his withdrawal and silent resentment. He knew deep inside that if he were honest he really hated his wife sometimes. How in the world would he ever change?

"Can you pick up Janie after school? I've got a church hostess meeting—we may have a late supper if it runs over," Michelle called to her husband.

"Another one?" Brian replied. "Didn't you just have one last week?"

"That was a children's department leadership conference."

"Whatever. I'll take the kids and we can eat out again."

Michelle could hear the disappointment and anger in his voice, but surely he understood. They both loved God and loved serving in the church, and yes, maybe she did overcommit her time and energy, but someone had to get the jobs done. "Besides," she reasoned, "if I weren't helping out at church, I'd be bored." But what about Brian's accusations that she used her tight schedule to avoid him and the kids? "That's nonsense," she'd argued back. "You know God comes first and then you and the children." Brian had merely shaken his head and walked out of the room.

Could her husband's charge be true? Did she need to change? Wasn't she merely paying the price required to serve God by serving His people? Maybe she could simply try to schedule her time more efficiently, making sure that she was home more. Inside, Michelle felt Brian's questions penetrate to the bottom of her conscience.

The truth was, she was terrified of facing the disappointment in her marriage, overwhelmed by what was required to be a good mother. She longed to relinquish her busyness and offer her heart to her family, but she just wasn't sure how.

Joanne listened intently to the voice on the other end of her cordless phone. She couldn't believe what she was hearing: the pastor's wife had been spotted coming out of the liquor store this week with not one, but two brown paper bags. Joanne's friend Vicki had seen it with her own eyes and was now relishing every detail over the phone. "You call Jenny and Cathy, and I'll call Deb," her friend instructed gleefully.

Joanne hung up and debated whether to spread the story or not. She didn't really want to, but Joanne suddenly felt the weight of her need to be part of the singles clique headed by Vicki. A couple of times early on she had gently rebuked Vicki for gossiping, but her new friend quickly turned on her: "Come on, Jo, it's not a big deal. What makes you so holier-than-thou?"

Joanne had felt the pangs of loneliness, the ones that used to come more frequently before she met Vicki. It made her feel like a silly schoolgirl, but she couldn't go back to that, to weekends at home in front of the television, shopping by herself. Vicki might be a gossip, but she was better than no one at all.

How could she ever confront Vicki and face being rejected? Why would God require that anyway? Didn't He provide Vicki and the other singles in answer to her prayers for friends? Why should she risk changing just because she felt a little guilty now and then? What would it take for her to love Vicki (as well as the ones being gossiped about) more than her selfish fear of being alone?

CHOICES

Can you relate to Steve's, Michelle's, and Joanne's dilemmas? How many times a day do you find yourself wrestling with choices? As Christians, don't we know how we are supposed to think, act, speak, and choose?

If you've faced the Christian life honestly, you know it's not that simple. While the Bible does provide us with principles for godly living, it rarely delivers specific formulas. God's Word is much less a rule book and more a thoughtful collection of stories and letters. For instance, I may know that as a Christian I'm called to be truthful and that I'm required to love my wife, but what does that look like when my wife asks, "Why don't you talk to me?" or, "You're so quiet. What are you thinking?" Do I dare tell the truth—that I'm incredibly disappointed that she doesn't love me in the ways I want to be loved? Isn't it more loving for me to keep quiet or to change the subject?

All of us, if we're honest, know the struggles of pursuing a life of faith. We're committed to Christ, we love God, and we want to share the Father's love with others. But we also struggle with what it means to be alive at the close of the twentieth century. Do we move to a bigger, nicer home just because we can afford to? Do I tell my spouse the truth when I know he or she will angrily make me pay? Do I compromise what I want in a mate or remain single? How do we decide which of our longings are legitimate and which are sinful And even if that seems clear, why do we still give in to things we know hurt God and others? Why does sin seem to dog us like a bloodhound?

"It's so frustrating," shares Tim, a thirty-two-year-old engineer. "I feel like I can't win. Either I let myself feel what I really feel, like wanting my wife to love me or wanting guys at church to befriend me, and then get incredibly disappointed, or I shut down and find myself angry and bitter. Either way I end up turning to things I hate, like overeating, to feel better. Where's God in all this? How in the world am I ever going to change? Should I simply quit wanting so much and just pray more? I feel like I'm waiting on some kind of cosmic zap from the Holy Spirit and then the Christian life will suddenly fall into place."

Debra, a single businesswoman in her late twenties, explains, "It's like this endless circle of wanting something—God, better relationships, personal change—being disappointed, finding some way to cope with it, usually sinful, and then turning over a new leaf and starting all over again."

A VICIOUS CYCLE

Sound familiar? This cycle of longing, sinning, and repenting seems inevitable if we're alive to the human condition and attuned to the Holy Spirit. We're created to long for more, to crave deep relationship with our Father and each other, to know our purposes and identities through knowing Christ; basically, we're born with a desire in our hearts for Heaven. However, sin remains just as inevitable, the stubborn remnant of human selfishness born out of Adam and Eve's choice in the garden.

But what about repentance? Shouldn't true repentance be more than a steppingstone in a futile cycle? Shouldn't a truly repentant heart display the fruit of loving God more passionately, the fruit of the Spirit? Why is it, then, that repentance as we often know and practice it takes us to a dead end?

While the props and circumstances may be different, the struggle of living a life of faith is nothing new. Virtually every person's story in the Bible recounts this tension with obstacles to faith, from Eve with the devilish serpent in Eden to the apostles doubting Christ's resurrection.

Paul addresses it best in his letter to the Romans as he candidly describes this struggle to grow beyond our sinful desires:

> What I don't understand about myself is that I decide one way, but then I act another, doing things I absolutely despise. So if I can't be trusted to figure out what is best for myself and then do it, it becomes obvious that God's command is necessary.
>
> But I need something *more*! For if I know the law but still can't keep it, and if the power of sin within me keeps sabotaging my best intentions, I obviously need help! I realize that I don't have what it takes. I can will it, but I can't *do* it. I decide to do good, but I don't *really* do it; I decide not to do bad, but then I do it anyway. My decisions, such as they are, don't result in actions. Something has gone wrong deep within me and gets the better of me every time.
>
> It happens so regularly that it's predictable. The moment I decide to do good, sin is there to trip me up. I truly delight in God's commands, but it's pretty obvious that not all of me joins in that delight. Parts of me covertly rebel, and just when I least expect it, they take charge.
>
> I've tried everything and nothing helps. I'm at the end

of my rope. Is there no one who can do anything for me? Isn't that the real question?" (Romans 7:15-24, MESSAGE)

---

1. Why do we often believe that Christians shouldn't struggle?
2. Describe a recent internal tug of war when you felt torn between doing what your self wanted to do and what you as a Christian wanted to do. How was it resolved?
3. What did you first expect the Christian life to be? How has it disappointed you? Surprised you?

While we may know intellectually the answer to Paul's question, "Is there no one who can do anything for me?" we don't own the answer in our bones, we don't live out of it. Part of the reason for this stems from the sheer frustration the cycle produces ("I've tried everything and nothing helps"). We're easily overwhelmed with what it means to live the Christian life and, more specifically, what it means to change, to be molded and chiseled more like Christ.

However, the difference between true repentance and relying on our own efforts (what we'll later define as "penance") usually boils down to our motives.

So often we want change for change's sake, a benchmark so we can feel better about ourselves, proof we're getting it right. And when self is the motivation at the center of our energy, then the cycle spirals in on itself, breeding anger (that we're not changing), fear (that we'll never change), and despair (that even God can't change us). So we end up with secrets, addictions, manipulations of others to get what we think we need to make us feel better, dark thoughts that maybe we're just not cut out to be a follower, a truster of Jesus. We become committed to relieving our pain through whatever sinful resources—an affair, overeating, alcoholism, selfishly withdrawing—seem to provide temporary comfort.

Or, we head toward the other extreme of pretending that our faith is stronger and richer than it is. This usually means denying that we're struggling with much of anything at all. We go through the motions of going to church, praying, helping others, but we know inside our faith is fragile, based more on rickety clichés than the bedrock Word of Life. When we're on this end of the spectrum, the same dark cycle swirls beneath our surface, the same commitment to feeling good about ourselves, merely disguised as the self-righteousness of our "spirituality."

In either extreme we're forced to admit that we can't change ourselves, that the process of spiritual change can't be reduced to a recipe. When we seek change for its own sake we become no more than Pharisees, legalists intent on beating the system. We end up thinking, "I'll follow God's rules, and if He doesn't come through for me, then I can justify myself." We end up back in the self-centered vortex of our vicious cycle.

Personally, most of my desires for spiritual change in the past have been so I could feel better about myself and struggle less. The truth is that *repentance for the sake of personal change is never true repentance*. In our age of self-help, recovery, counseling, and therapy, most of us come up against the tension of wanting to feel better (about ourselves and life) and wanting to be more godly (glorifying God through the struggles of our lives).

So how do we pursue God while not denying how we feel? How do we break out of the extremes? How can we move toward the middle ground of the spectrum, toward a place where we don't deny our struggles and yet don't demand relief through the comforts of sin? What does it look like to truly repent?

COMING TO OUR SENSES

True repentance begins by taking an honest inventory within ourselves, owning up to our sinful condition as well as our longing for more. Let's consider this by taking a look at one of the best-known stories of repentance, the prodigal son. You'll recall that after squandering his premature inheritance on the good life, the prodigal resorted to slopping hogs for his survival. "And he was longing to fill his stomach with the pods that the swine were eating, and no one was giving anything to him" (Luke 15:16).

For me, growing up on a farm in Tennessee, it's a graphic picture. I shudder to think about being so desperately hungry that I would ever eat from the pails I used to empty in a big, muddy trough. Usually the scraps had accumulated over several days: moldy bread, spoiled meats, cornhusks, and rotten apple cores. On a hot summer day the stench alone often made me nauseated. While the prodigal's pig-food may not have been exactly like mine, it was no less repulsive.

> "But when he came to his senses, he said, 'How many of my father's hired men have more than enough bread, but I am dying here with hunger! I will get up and go to my father, and will say to him, "Father, I have sinned against heaven, and in your sight; I am no longer worthy to be called your son; make me as one of your hired men."'" (Luke 15:17-19)

"When he came to his senses." What does it mean for us to come to our senses? How often I've found myself trying desperately to find a way to make more money, write more books, seek deeper relationships. These aren't bad in themselves, but when I'm making them more important than God, when I'm seeking them as an early inheritance so I can feel good about the way life's under my control, then I've turned away from my Father. Rarely do I want to recognize my idolatrous pig-food for what it is. But I am aware of my dissatisfaction with the way I live my life avoiding my Father. So how do you and I come to our senses?

Before we consider this question, I believe it's important to remind you of what I expressed in my introduction: true repentance never begins as a conscious effort of will on our parts, merely a switch waiting to be flipped. If you're reading this book, you're probably well aware that you can't make it happen on your own. In fact, trying too hard usually leads us into the old cycles of denial, defeat, and despair. Instead, genuine repentance is usually much more sublime, a shift inside from our hunger to feed ourselves to our longing to be nourished by the Father. However, keep in mind that even though we can't repent simply by trying harder, we are not to give up and wait passively for the Holy Spirit or some outside force to zap us.

So while we can't analyze the prodigal's process of coming to his senses for the sake of imitation, a formula that stimulates change for us, we should notice two crucial aspects of his awakening. The prodigal realizes both his *value* and his *need*, and the inextricable link between himself and his father. First, he recognizes he was created for more than pig slop; he becomes dissatisfied with the counterfeits of life that sin provides.

> A return to God the Father begins with the recognition that sin is degrading. As the rebellious son sat slumped in a pigpen, he had to face that eating the food fed to pigs was beneath a Hebrew, who would not even eat pork, let alone pig slop.[1]

In thinking through our value to our Father, first consider how far short the prodigal falls in estimating his worth. "I am no longer worthy to be called your son; make me as one of your hired men." By realizing that even as wretched as he is, he deserves better than slop, the prodigal estimates his father's goodness. The son's worst-case scenario is to return, face his dad's justifiable wrath, and become a servant, a hired hand.

As I think about this story, my worst-case scenario is usually far worse. Even though it doesn't follow logically with the theology in my head, my heart fears God as if He were a vindictive tyrant. So when I think about leaving my slop and returning to Him, I imagine the shame and contempt He will pour on me. I'll walk up the path to the house, stop Him from His busy schedule, and He'll laugh, "I knew you'd be back, you worthless son." From there He'll become a cruel judge conducting a line-item audit of all the sordid ways I spent my inheritance, all the sinful ways I've tried to make life work without Him. And you know what? He has every right to do this.

The prodigal's realization of this, as well as mine and yours, is essential. "I've sinned against heaven, and in your sight." He owns the horror of his selfishness, the terrifying realization that he went his own way and crashed, and more importantly that he trampled his father's heart in the process. He not only recognizes his physical need for food, but he realizes his need for forgiveness, his need to face the consequences of his self-absorption. Thus, the awareness of his value is tempered with an awareness of his sinful state, keeping him from demanding that the father take him back. Likewise, he can face the consequences of facing his sin because he has some idea of what it means to have a father who loves him.

But consider how wrong both the prodigal and we are in our feeble estimations of our Father's goodness:

> "But while he was still a long way off, his father saw
> him, and felt compassion for him, and ran and embraced
> him and kissed him."

While the prodigal stammers out his apology, the father calls for jewelry and dress clothes, and tearfully announces a celebration like no other. "For this son of mine was dead, and has come to life again; he was lost, and has been found."

Ponder the inexplicable goodness of such a father. Christ Himself reminds us of our incomprehension of the Father's goodness:

> "What man is there among you, when his son shall ask
> him for a loaf, will give him a stone? Or if he shall ask
> for a fish, he will not give him a snake, will he? If you
> then, being evil, know how to give good gifts to your
> children, how much more shall your Father who is in
> heaven give what is good to those who ask Him!"
> (Matthew 7:9-11)

Back to the prodigal's story—notice how the son responds to his father's display of goodness. The line is concise, but crucial: "And they began to be merry." Whether the prodigal wrestled with self-contempt, suspicion that his father was setting him up, or incredulity, we don't know. If he was human, though, he probably did. But he didn't stay there. He accepted the incomprehensible gift of his father's love, the same gift offered to all of us in the offering of Christ and the ongoing gift of sanctification through God's presence in our day-to-day lives. But why isn't change that easy? What if I can't relate to the prodigal's turnaround?

As I write this, I'm well aware that some of you reading will be moved, that these words may be used by the Spirit to stir a heartfelt longing and shift deep within. Others of you might react with, "Well, that's nice," or "I hadn't thought of the story quite that way." Still others will feel nothing at all, a numb distance. And still others will feel rage: "How can I trust in God's goodness when my life's so hard?" or "I'm doing all I can, so why haven't I changed?" Those are important questions and must be asked, but we must be willing to ask them against an openness, like the prodigal's, to look at our own sinful need and our own redeemed value. Otherwise we end up feeling just as angry and justified as the prodigal's older brother.

THE REST OF THE STORY

Resentment

> "Now his older son was in the field, and when he came and approached the house, he heard music and dancing. And he summoned one of the servants and began inquiring what these things might be. And he said to him, 'Your brother has come, and your father has killed the fattened calf, because he has received him back safe and sound.' But he became angry, and was not willing to go in; and his father came out and began entreating him. But he answered and said to his father, 'Look! For so

many years I have been serving you, and I have never
neglected a command of yours; and yet you have never
given me a kid that I might be merry with my friends;
but when this son of yours came, who has devoured
your wealth with harlots, you killed the fattened calf for
him.'" (Luke 15:25-30)

Maybe you have difficulty putting yourself in the prodigal's
shoes. Maybe you've grown up in a Christian home, known our
Lord a long time, served tirelessly at church, given yourself to
every Christian endeavor that comes your way. You can't really
relate to the overt misbehavior of the younger son. You can't
recall any rebellious escapades—no affairs, no addictions, no
pursuits for your own pleasure. Or maybe you could relate to
the prodigal at one time, back when you first accepted Christ's
invitation, but now it seems foggy and distant. Now it's hard not
to feel the frustration of the Christian life and what it requires.

Certainly all these feelings are encompassed in the older
son's response. He feels incredibly justified in making his charges
against the father, indicting him on the son's perceived merit
system. The father owes him. The injustice of the spoiled brat—
"this son of yours," not even fit to be called his brother—coming home to a grand celebration while he's been home all along
toiling away! It's not fair. He deserves more.

If you're honest, can't you relate? At some level, don't we
all want to demand guarantees from God? "Lord, I'll do my part
for You, I'll do everything a good Christian man or woman should
do, if You come through for me." Ironically enough, we would
all like to participate in the very merit system that would kill us
if we were under it.

The Merit System
Let's take a hard look at that merit system. Exactly what would
we get if we were treated "fairly"? Would things go our way more
often? Would we get what we think we deserve: a bigger house,
a car that runs, a devoted spouse, a healthy family, independent

wealth, good friends, a faith-filled church? We must make an important distinction here. While we have deep soul longings for love, intimacy, comfort, and joy, they reflect our need for God, not our equality with Him. He created us as men and women in the image of His own being. His first creations, Adam and Eve, were designed for a direct relationship of harmonious fellowship in the garden. After they rebelliously disobeyed, they activated the sinful nature that comes as part of having the will to choose God or self. Even after they left the garden, they were forced to live with the knowledge of its beauty and grieve the lost relationship with their Creator. We still suffer both major aftereffects today: as redeemed image-bearers, we have Heaven planted in our hearts, a yearning for intimacy with our Father, and yet we also know the selfishness of our sinful natures.

As selfish beings, we often blur the distinction between legitimate, even holy, *longings*, which require suffering and grief to sustain, and *demands*, self-directed ultimatums that justify our sins and take us out of the pain of our longings. But we must realize that we have no platform from which to demand anything of God. Nothing. Those who would claim to be without sin automatically commit the sins of pride, deception, and hypocrisy. As Paul explained to the Romans, it doesn't matter how good we think we are, or how hard we try to follow God's law; we're still stuck with a sinful nature. We're inherently selfish. At our very best, when things are going well with family and finances, and we sense dramatic growth in our walk with Christ, we still need God's forgiveness. We will never not need Him. Too often, most of us are aware of needing God's help for our lives to work or to be better people, but we overlook the inherent neediness of our souls simply because we exist as selfish beings born into a fallen world.

Consider the Old Testament offerings required by God in Leviticus. The Israelites were required to make various offerings to pay for their sins before Yahweh, the Holy and Righteous God. The book of the Law goes into minute detail on the selection, preparation, and execution of each kind of sacrifice—burnt offerings, grain offerings, peace offerings. Most of these offerings had to be made as a result of particular violations—stealing, lying, adultery, idolatry, etc.—and were called trespass offerings. But sacrifices were also required for unintentional and unaware sins. These sin offerings, obviously, had to be made continually since some selfishness could always be discerned even in the best motives.

Facing Our Neediness
Our Father, in His goodness, engineered a permanent solution for us to the problem of the unfulfillable law—the sacrifice of a part of Himself to take our place. While this sacrifice of Christ on two crossbeams of wood permanently fulfilled all of the penalty requirements of the Law, and thus our need to make offerings in order to know God, too often we forget our inherent neediness. It's easy to make a shopping list of various sins we commit on a daily basis—I didn't love my wife as well as I could, I told a white lie to a friend, I failed to give money to the church—but it's much harder to face the ugliness of our sinful nature.

As long as we can stay in the realm of listing our sins, asking for God's forgiveness, and trying harder to be obedient, we can manage our life pretty well. But as long as we stay in this surface level of sinfulness, we will never need or taste the depths of God's grace. This doesn't mean we should go out and sin really big to test that grace. We've sinned and are sinning really big right now. Whether our sin is obvious like the prodigal son's pleasure binge or more subtle like the insidious, angry self-centeredness of the elder son, we all need and long for our Father's forgiving embrace.

Notice that the father's grace is offered just as generously to the older son as it is to the younger:

> "My child, you have always been with me, and all that is mine is yours. But we had to be merry and rejoice, for this brother of yours was dead and has begun to live, and was lost and has been found." (Luke 15:31-32)

The father doesn't defend himself, he doesn't retaliate, and he doesn't even bristle at his eldest's bitter hatefulness. He responds with the same tenderness that compassionately embraced his vagabond wild son earlier. The father reminds his jealous, justified son of the grace extended and accepted with his brother's return, a cause for great celebration.

It is an unexpected, grace-filled response. It illuminates that while the older son has not disobediently wandered from the house, he has gradually hardened his heart and wandered just as far from home.

The parable is left open-ended; Jesus doesn't tell us if or how the older son responded to his father's tender mercy. And that, of course, was much of the point in His telling it for the benefit of the Pharisees and scribes who approached Him grumbling, "This man receives sinners and eats with them" (Luke 15:2).

Most people have no difficulty recognizing the prodigal son as the tax gatherers and sinners who eagerly received Jesus, nor seeing the older brother as symbolic of the Pharisees. But we must realize that we all contain the motives of both sons within ourselves as well. Perhaps we can identify with one more than the other, but we're all forced to contend with what it means to continually turn from our sin—both overt misbehavior and subtle, inherent selfishness—and return to our Father.

---

4. Are you more like the younger son or the older son in the way you relate to God? Why do you think so?
5. Imagine you're a prodigal returning home after sinfully squandering your early inheritance. How would you expect the father to handle you? How would you like the father to handle you?

WHY WE AVOID GRACE

So we want to come to our senses. We genuinely, desperately long to know and love our Abba Father. The sinful ways we use to try to make our lives work suddenly seem futile, shallow, even silly. Why would I want to eat slop when I was created to be a child of the King and dine at His table? Why would I even try to justify myself to God and demand His favor when He offers me the riches of His grace? When the contrast is that sharp, it seems insane not to come home to the Father. So even if we're willing to accept grace, what keeps our hearts hardened out in the fields? What keeps my heart deadened to be content with slop?

Quite simply, pride. Like the prodigal, we're forced to admit, "I've sinned against heaven and in your sight; I am no longer worthy to be called your child." Turning from our troughs and returning home to a father whom we have legitimately wronged and wounded requires deep humility. We're forced to face up to consequences, fears, and shame. When we acknowledge the selfishness of our actions, we can no longer deny the impact on our relationship with God and others. We hurt God in our childish rebellions; we damage others in our selfish indifference to anyone but ourselves. Logically, facing the very justified wrath of God and anger or hurt of others is not pleasant.

We deserve punishment. Shame then infuses our hearts as the weight of this settles in; we do indeed deserve punishment because we knew better, but preferred to take our chances on our abilities nonetheless. Our pride is devastated when this selfish gamble fails in futility. We're back to needing God's forgiveness as well as others'—perhaps even more visibly than we did when we started. We are forced to strip ourselves of pride and return to God in the nakedness of humility.

We're also forced to acknowledge God's righteousness and goodness, two traits that only highlight our sinfulness. First, by admitting our sin, we agree that God is without fault, that He has every right to disown us and leave us on our own. Second, we appeal to the goodness manifest in His love offering of Christ's sacrificial death on the cross. Such humility melts the prideful ice of our hearts and leads to a current of sorrow. Repentance then rises out of the recognition and admission that our sin is awful. Our souls break with the weight of our selfishness, the offensive rebellion that reeks with the stench of idolatry. Out of this brokenness we sorrow deeply for the ways we hurt God and others. (Consider how this runs antithetical to the messages of our society, which tell us to work hard, to look good, to conceal flaws, to shift blame to others, to feel good about ourselves at any cost.)

CONSEQUENCES OF GRACE

This kind of brokenness is far from self-flagellation and pharisaic martyrdom. It is not an I'm-lower-than-dirt, please-have-mercy-on-me-Lord kind of self-pitying sorrow. There's something pure and clean about it, as if we're willing to own the debris of our selfishness, ask God to drain it out of our hearts, and face Him in the still clarity of our hunger for Him. Out of this we hear the call or glimpse a vision of who we are created to be. We see and believe that we're created for more, that we are redeemed men and women, children of the King. We face the truth deep inside that we know we were created for more than a futile system of dos and don'ts—more than our own selfish pursuits, more than this world offers. We believe God is a merciful Father lovingly leading us as His own children, that even in the midst of the hardest things life dishes out—lost jobs, children with leukemia, loneliness, rape—He's still all powerful in His goodness.

But such a faith feels as though it requires too much. In fact, such a conflict between our desire to trust God and the urgency of hard circumstances often leads us in at least two strong directions. Either we resign ourselves to the futile cycle described above (relieving our pain through sin and denial—the prodigal's rebellion or the elder son's self-justified righteousness) or we become convicted by a hope far bigger than ourselves.

Such a conviction requires a turning away from self, and dependence on God and His grace. Perhaps there's no simpler definition of repentance than *the life process of turning away from self and toward our Father*. This kind of faith requires believing that our Creator is authoring a masterpiece tapestry of all our realities beyond the mere landscape of what we can see and feel. When we're committed to knowing, loving, and trusting God beyond our circumstances, then we begin movement in a different direction. We realize our selfish agendas of feeling safe, comfortable, and happy all the time are not priorities from God's perspective. He's committed to a much deeper, much more radical love of our souls. Our transformation into Christlikeness (sanctification) takes precedence over our comfort and convenience.

But such a shift, whether a small tremor or large quake, comes with a steep price: suffering. When we look to God because we were created for Him, by Him, to seek Him passionately with all our being rather than believing that He should serve as a cosmic problem-solver, then we begin the kind of suffering required by true repentance. This honest inventory faces the ugliness in ourselves (our need for God because of our inherent self-centeredness) while simultaneously embracing that we are created for more (our value as redeemed men and women created in our Father's image). Paradoxically, when we realize that we are not the point, that knowing and loving God is the focus, then we become willing to suffer living between the tension of our lingering selfish nature and our new redeemed heart.

Part of suffering this tension means looking honestly at how we hurt others out of our sinfulness. If we indeed are not the point, then we can begin the slow and often painful process of looking at how we affect others. "It wasn't until I realized how deeply I was hurting my wife that I began to recognize my need for God," states Jim, a forty-three-year-old management consultant. "No matter what we argued about, I always turned it back on her—it could always be her fault. I was destroying her because I wasn't willing to take responsibility for my selfishness."

Examining our impact on others means more than simply asking how we've hurt them and then offering a quick "I'm sorry." It means that we're willing to own our sin against them, the times we lash out in anger and say harsh words that we know will scald others' hearts, the times we withdraw and offer next to nothing and feel justified because at least there's no overt damage.

Do you dare even ask your spouse for honest feedback about your relationship? How do your children perceive you as a parent? What would your friends say about you? Your coworkers? Are you willing to hear their feedback and not defend or justify yourself, but to feel the weight of how you hurt them? *A repentant heart experiences deep sorrow for the pain inflicted on others by selfishness rather than feeling sorry for oneself.*

While we'll look more closely at issues of restitution and brokenness in chapters 3 and 7, for now keep in mind that a genuinely repentant heart experiences deep sorrow and grief for pain inflicted on others rather than feeling self-pity. Like most of the repentance process, this aspect cannot be reduced to a contrived formula. Rather it grows out of a willingness to see the ugliness of our sin and turn to God's merciful forgiveness and then offer the same grace to others. We become less concerned with getting ourselves off the hook and more focused on knowing our Father's goodness and shining His love through the prism of our hearts. We become willing to become loving fathers who run down the paths of others' lives, stunning them with the embrace of our Creator's goodness. Those who are forgiven little, love little. Those who are forgiven much, love much (Luke 7:47).

THE ONGOING STRUGGLE

Think back to Paul's question in Romans: "Is there no one who can do anything for me?" Consider how deep and passionate your yearning is for intimacy with your Savior, the One who saved you and continues to save you from the futility of the ridiculous merit systems we often put ourselves through. As Paul explains,

> The answer, thank God, is that Jesus Christ can and does. He acted to set things right in this life of contradictions where I want to serve God with all my heart and mind, but am pulled by the influence of sin to do something totally different. (Romans 7:25, MESSAGE)

What will sustain us to continue forward, to view repentance as a daily, lifetime process and not as a one-shot choice or cosmic zap outside ourselves? Ultimately, God's goodness, manifest through His Son, Christ. Our part involves receiving, being joyfully stunned in a celebration of grace, and living gratefully out of such grace in our Father. Toward that end we can face the legitimacy of our longings, fears, and emotions; acknowledge our lifelong inclination toward selfishness and sin; and move forward with our eyes set on God and whom He calls us to become. In other words, we can come to our senses, realizing our need and our value, and being convicted by a vision of the way our Father sees us.

JOURNALING THE JOURNEY

As you read this book, I encourage and challenge you to keep a journal of your thoughts and feelings. Even if you've never thought of yourself as a writer, don't let that be an excuse. Simply record your responses, questions, feelings, and desires as honestly as possible. Don't worry about punctuation, grammar, or spelling; no one's going to grade this. In fact, no one needs to see it (or even know about it) but you.

This journal should be your place to think about God, your relationship with Him, and what it means for you to draw closer to Him. At the end of each chapter, I'll offer some suggested questions or cues to ponder in your journal. Keep in mind, though, that these are only suggestions. Feel free to explore this material and your life however you wish.

As a catalyst for your own journaling journey, in each chapter I will also include a brief entry from my own journals in which I struggle with my life and the material I'm writing about here.

From My Journal

I'm starting yet another journal, a place to think about my life and what it means to wrestle with God, wrestle with knowing Him. I feel so overwhelmed right now, so caught up in the busy-

ness of teaching and counseling, let alone loving my wife and new daughter. I feel like something's going on in me—of course it is—but it feels distant, far away, a lone coin drifting in the bottom of a deep fountain. I'm tired of feeling the way I do, like God's part of my life, but only in the periphery, like I've had Him on the phone and kept Him on hold for months. I want to talk to Him, to share struggles, but it feels too scary, uncertain. When I pray now it feels forced. So maybe I shouldn't pray? I don't think that's it either. I just know I want more from Him. I want to change, to know more about the man He wants me to be. I don't want things to depend so much on the way I feel.

For Your Journal

Now to get you started, consider why you bought this book. What were you hoping it would be? How would you like it to help you? What's your impression so far of what's been said about repentance? Where do you see yourself? How do you feel? Are you disappointed, angry, frustrated, encouraged, excited, frightened, anxious, impatient? Try to describe your present place with God as honestly as possible. How would you like your life to be different by the time you finish this book?

2

TEMPTATIONS

If you've ever tried to diet, then you can immediately remember a very tangible temptation. It seems every time I try to lose a few pounds, I'm bombarded with my favorite fat-drenched foods—double chocolate chunk ice cream, French fries, eggs Benedict, guacamole and chips. Suddenly every box and can on the grocery shelf lunges at me with the promise of delicious taste and inconsequential calories. But as we all know, the latter doesn't exist this side of Heaven.

While overeating is a serious struggle for some, it's probably not what heads our top ten temptations (but it's certainly on my list). Usually the temptations we wrestle with have deeper roots, cutting into our very beings. Things like lust, fantasy, pornography, perversions. Relational struggles like jealousy, envy, gossip, withdrawal, and subtle hatred. *In fact, most of the things with which we struggle reflect our attempt to be taken out of difficult emotional landscapes, places of pain, hurt, anger, frustration, boredom, sadness, and grief.* Either we seek to alleviate such pain and feel better through some self-made resource, or we seek to remove ourselves from feeling altogether, which serves the same purpose. In either case, we're refusing to live in the tension of this fallen world where hurting, crying, and grieving are inherent parts of our human condition.

FLIGHT FROM PAIN

Steve sat in his office and stared out the window. Although it wasn't even noon yet, the work on his desk had piled up; most of the projects were his single-handedly. A pall of loneliness crept over him like the clouds' shifting shadows on the plaza below.

He thought of his wife, Anne, and the way they'd both been so busy lately. He thought about the way they rarely ever spent time alone anymore, and while it was justifiable given his overtime and their three kids, he realized he missed her. But it seemed unlikely that they'd be able to connect on any level other than "What's for dinner?" and "Did you change the oil in the van?" for quite a while.

He missed having friends, brothers to confide in, play basketball with, go to lunch with. Steve thought about calling his friend Dan from his small group, or John from his Sunday school class. They were probably pretty busy, though. He figured he really shouldn't expect anything from them.

Driving off to lunch, Steve found himself taking a familiar route of back streets and side roads until he finally parked behind a large warehouse. Inside were all kinds of magazines and videos with strong men and beautiful women. He hated himself for this; it was not what he wanted. Yet, he came here almost instinctively, on auto-pilot. Despite his ambivalence, his attraction and repulsion, his loneliness would at least be alleviated for the rest of the day. Maybe then he could get some work done.

Michelle found herself with two free hours on Friday afternoon. On one hand, she could spend the time just relaxing until the kids got home from school. She could make a cup of tea, sit down with her Bible and her journal, and just think about her relationship with the Lord, her marriage, her children. Michelle shuddered, though, as she recalled the last time she'd spent her time that way. It ended up being so painful. Deep down she knew she was afraid of God—He was so unpredictable, so uncontrollable. And what about her marriage? Brian kept challenging her to spend more time with him and the kids rather than at church or the kids' school. She was terrified of that. What if Brian saw how inept she really was? What if the kids saw that she didn't always know what to do?

No, those two hours would not be spent that way. She dialed the church office and chatted with Betty, the receptionist. Sure enough, some fliers needed folding for bulletin insertion, and then there was a wedding reception planning meeting that could certainly benefit from her expertise. Michelle wrote a neatly detailed note for the kids when they got home from school and reminded them of the snacks in the fridge she had prepared for them. Wasn't helping down at the church better than moping at home and feeling sorry for herself?

Michelle and Steve both long for something deeper, but fear facing what lurks between them and that deeper yearning. Thus, the temptations they face are compounded into ripe opportunities because they provide diversion, escape, withdrawal, and avoidance. Such temptations will always pop up, sometimes predictably, but usually when we can be surprised amidst vulnerability. While we may long for Heaven and yearn for the time when we will be with our Father forever, for now we must realize that facing temptation should be expected.

Indeed, the fact that we're struggling only points to the tension between our flesh and spirit, the stress of being a selfishly inclined man or woman redeemed by the Creator through the power of Christ. In her classic *The Christian's Secret of a Happy Life*, Hannah Whithall Smith encourages,

> And the very power of your temptations, dear Christian, may perhaps be one of the strongest proofs that you

really are in the land you have been seeking to enter, because they are temptations peculiar to that land. You must never allow them to cause you to question the fact of your having entered it.[1]

TEMPTATION: THE PRICE OF FREEDOM

Temptation is ultimately an inherent byproduct of one of God's greatest gifts to us—free will. Rather than creating us as programmable androids, God desired relationship with other beings similar to Himself, beings who feel, think, create, and love. This goal necessitates a certain level of autonomy. Any true relationship involves choices on the part of both parties to choose the other. Choices involve alternatives, and that means we could choose not to have a personal relationship with our heavenly Father. And even having chosen one, we still vacillate in our willingness to trust Him.

In fact, Adam and Eve wasted no time in exercising this gift of free will. Compounded by the serpent's deceit, our first parents' struggle to maintain their relationship with God in the garden or to explore new possibilities of becoming just like Him expressed itself in the simple choice of obedience or disobedience. Let's look at this life-changing moment.

Now the serpent was more crafty than any beast of the field which the LORD God had made. And he said to the woman, "Indeed, has God said, 'You shall not eat from any tree of the garden'?" And the woman said to the serpent, "From the fruit of the trees of the garden we may eat; but from the fruit of the tree which is in the middle of the garden, God has said, 'You shall not eat from it or touch it, lest you die.'" And the serpent said to the woman, "You surely shall not die! For God knows that in the day you eat from it your eyes will be opened, and you will be like God, knowing good and evil." When the woman saw that the tree was good for food, and that it was a delight to the eyes, and that the tree was desirable to make one wise, she took from its fruit and ate; and she gave also to her husband with her, and he ate. Then the eyes of both of them were opened, and they knew that they were naked; and they sewed fig leaves together and made themselves loin coverings. (Genesis 3:1-7)

Notice the way the serpent knows exactly which buttons to push, whom to address, and how to tantalize by perverting the truth. He begins with a bold overstatement, "Indeed, has God said, 'You shall not eat from any tree of the garden'?" Well aware that God has placed rules only around the tree of knowledge (and implicitly the tree of life), Satan craftily exaggerates this into an unbearable edict in an attempt to portray the Creator as an intolerable tyrant. The implicit message in his opening question goes something like this: "You mean to say that God has forbidden you from eating the delicious fruit from all these beautiful fruit trees? That's certainly unreasonable and selfish of Him."

When Eve clarifies that they may eat of any tree except the one in the middle of the garden (and one is certainly a far cry from all), then the stage is set for the serpent to deliver his lie. Even though there is no prohibition on all fruit, still, since one is off limits, then by implication we should perceive God as unfair. And if God's rule seems unfair, then why should we trust Him? With doubt planted in Eve's (and Adam's) mind, the snake extends his exaggeration to a blatant lie: God is not good and has lied to you in order to suppress your true potential of power and awareness. *If you quit playing by His rules, then you will in fact be just like Him.*

This is, in essence, the persuasion of deceit the Enemy uses on us today. It's virtually the only weapon he has, and his only joy is sustaining the lie as long as possible in order to blind us momentarily to our birthright as redeemed image-bearers. He still knows what buttons to push to get us to question and hopefully doubt God's goodness and sovereignty.

Let's return to our close-up of Eve and Adam for a moment. With the cruel irony of the serpent's words—"You surely shall not die! For God knows that in the day you eat from it your eyes will be opened, and you will be like God, knowing good and evil"—still hissing in her mind, Eve then makes a crucial error in judgment. *Basically, she trusts her own judgment more than God's.* Since God cannot be trusted in light of His rule about the tree (or fill in the blank with your own area of doubting God's goodness: a painful marriage, the death of a child, a crippling disease, a sexual struggle), then we suddenly believe that our own understanding is all we have.

Notice how Eve filters the evidence through her own judgment then: the tree looks good for food, it is a delight to the eyes, it is desirable to make one wise. She relies on the frailty of human reasoning tickled by the lies of the serpent to make a choice for or against God. We know how she chooses and how Adam then chooses just as we know how very often we choose the same.

---

1. How would you define temptation in your own words? What pictures instantly come to mind?

Well aware of the hefty price to be paid for His creation's free will, God mercifully launched the plan that would redeem the selfishness set in motion by Adam and Eve's choice. Over hundreds of years and through generations of life stories, the Father relentlessly pursued His people despite their wanderings. He provided the Law as a means of highlighting His holiness and their (and our) unrighteousness. Without discarding His holy standard, God then provided the means to bridge the chasm between Himself and humankind. He sent His only Son forth from the heavenly Trinity to be born as a baby, minister as a man, and die as the only worthy propitiation for the sin of a selfish world. The capstone of His loving pursuit is this grace manifest through the unfathomable sacrifice of Christ on the cross.

So presently, once we accept Christ's free gift, we no longer have to struggle with temptation—right? While we may wish it so, the truth, of course, remains that we will struggle until we reach Heaven. However, if that's the case, and it is, then how do we resist temptation and seek God? What does it mean to struggle well?

STRUGGLING WELL

One of the best pictures of struggling well, and the sharpest contrast to our previous close-up of Adam and Eve, is Jesus coming off a fast in the desert, tempted by Satan himself.

Next Jesus was taken into the wild by the Spirit for the Test. The Devil was ready to give it. Jesus prepared for the Test by fasting forty days and forty nights. That left him, of course, in a state of extreme hunger, which the Devil took advantage of in the first test: "Since you are God's Son, speak the word that will turn these stones into loaves of bread."

Jesus answered by quoting Deuteronomy: "It takes more than bread to stay alive. It takes a steady stream of words from God's mouth."

For the second test the Devil took him to the Holy City. He sat him on top of the Temple and said, "Since you are God's Son, jump." The Devil goaded him by quoting Psalm 91: "He has placed you in the care of angels. They will catch you so that you won't so much as stub your toe on a stone."

Jesus countered with another citation from Deuteronomy: "Don't you dare test the Lord your God."

For the third test, the Devil took him on the peak of a huge mountain. He gestured expansively, pointing out all the earth's kingdoms, how glorious they all were. Then he said, "They're yours—lock, stock, and barrel. Just go down on your knees and worship me, and they're yours."

Jesus' refusal was curt: "Beat it, Satan!" He backed his rebuke with a third quotation from Deuteronomy: "Worship the Lord your God, and only him. Serve him with absolute single-heartedness."

The Test was over. The Devil left. And in his place, angels! Angels came and took care of Jesus' needs. (Matthew 4:1-11, MESSAGE)

Led by the Spirit

The first thing that strikes me about this passage is that Jesus was led by the *Spirit* to be tempted by Satan. How often do we think of the Holy Spirit as leading us into temptation? Doesn't that contradict our instruction to pray, "Lead us not into temptation" from our Lord's prayer in Matthew 6? It offers contrast, but not contradiction. God desires us to be sanctified into the likeness of Christ, not to be comfortable by avoiding any struggle or temptation. It's one thing for us to request God's presence to help us endure temptations, to protect us from ourselves and Satan, and another thing for us to demand that God remove us from hard circumstances involving temptation.

When we consider that the Spirit led Jesus to be tested, we should keep in mind the context and timing: immediately following Christ's baptism. Jesus went from hearing, "This is My beloved Son, in whom I am well-pleased" (Matthew 3:17) to literally facing the taunts of Satan. So often we go from the worshipful intensity of a mountaintop connection with our Lord to the bottom of the valley of our greatest struggles.

If it is true that sometimes the Spirit leads us to be tested, then we must also keep in mind other truth contained in Scripture: "No temptation has overtaken you but such as is common to man; and God is faithful, who will not allow you to be tempted beyond what you are able, but with the temptation will provide the way of escape also, that you may be able to endure it" (1 Corinthians 10:13). It would seem that sometimes God allows temptations, even has the Spirit lead us into them, for our ultimate good, to build our character, to reveal His character at a deeper level, to display the wonder of His glory. Keep in mind, however, that this is very different from our choosing to face temptation, which usually involves our testing God or wanting to be tantalized by sin.

Temptation insofar as it is an act of the evil one arising out of his envy and hatred is certainly evil. Insofar as it is the good things of the world enticing our disintegrated nature to act in insubordination, it is not good. But for those who love God, all things work together unto good. The challenge [of temptations] can make us grow, give us fuller insight, make us more like our Lord and Master, who struggled with temptation from the days in the wilderness till he hung naked on the cross and was buffeted with the cry: If you be the Son, come down.[2]

Physical Temptation

When we look at Christ face to face with Satan in the desert, we notice three different varieties of temptation offered. First, notice that Satan chooses to act on the physical: Jesus' hunger. Just as repentant movement begins for the prodigal with physical hunger, so, too, does temptation often strike our physical needs and longings. With this strategy there's an immediate, even urgent, opportunity. The immediate gratification of abating the physical need momentarily outweighs a higher commitment or promise. Consider Esau selling his birthright to Jacob for a mere bowl of stew. In his moment of intense hunger, something as lofty and intangible as a birthright didn't seem to matter much.

So it is with us. Often it's hard to remember the power of God's love and redemption of us when we're feeling hungry, tired, depressed, or sexually aroused. It's much easier to focus on the physical sensations of our bodies and satisfy them immediately, regardless of the cost.

But our Father wants more for us. He wants us to be committed to Him beyond the physical sensations of our own bodies. Of course, that does not mean He doesn't want us to eat, sleep, feel, etc., but it does mean that He doesn't want us controlled by such drives and impulses. Notice how Jesus rebukes Satan by appealing to a principle higher, more essential to His being (and ours): The words of God provide more ultimate nourishment than mere bread.

Attack on Our Identity

The second test involves plucking at another deep chord within: *identity*. From the top of the temple, Satan challenges, "Since you are God's Son, jump!" He uses circular reasoning (Scripture about the power of God's Son) to reinforce his dare.

How often we are buffeted by Satan's attacks on our identities as redeemed men and women. The Enemy hits at both parts here: our identities as people saved by God's grace through His Son's blood, and our identities as male and female image-bearers of our Creator. Often the Devil's attacks on our identity in Christ are blatant. He works to convince us that we're not really saved, that God isn't really powerful enough to forgive us (maybe everyone else, but not us), that we're too bad, too dangerous and wicked. The Enemy tries to isolate us and let our own self-absorption instill fear to the point where we live outside of what we already have, who we're redeemed to be.

The other attack, on our gender identity, is equally insidious. For men this attack often expresses itself sexually, through addictions, masturbation, pornography, perversions, affairs, fantasies. Satan seeks to render us men impotent as powerful image-bearers of our Father, moving boldly into the lives of those around us with His strength, love, and grace. This might express itself through any number of scenarios—passivity, procrastination, busyness, or withdrawal.

For women, Satan's attack on gender often takes a more relational route. Rather than being soul-nourishers who invite and offer warmth and intimacy, reflectors of beauty and mercy, women find themselves desiring to control their circumstances to ensure they will not be hurt. Often they become hard, tough, or distant, convinced that they have nothing to offer, convinced they are not women of beauty and substance. They might be tempted to gossip, lie, manipulate, and seductively control.

Christ battled the Devil's challenge to His identity by exercising faith. He reminded His enemy once again of a higher principle from God's Word: "Don't you dare test the Lord your God." In other words, Jesus chose to believe His Father's Word about

His identity—that He really is the Son of God and doesn't have to prove it because of a bully's taunt. If we dared to live out of who we really are as redeemed image-bearers and who God calls us to be, I believe we would consistently find the courageous faith to respond as Jesus responded.

Temptation to Worship
Finally, the third test involved power, authority, and worship—perhaps, bottom line, the core of our hearts and souls. Think for a moment about what Jesus was offered here, the kingdoms of the world with all their glory.

Without doubting the veracity of Scripture, I think too often we consider this incident as fable or allegory, a story so well-known that it, including the temptation, loses some of its power. It's hard to imagine all the kingdoms of the world, all the wealth and power, prestige and celebrity, being fully at our disposal. Most days I settle for daydreaming about winning the lottery or writing a best seller, paying off the mortgage, and traveling around the world in first-class style. Think of your wildest fantasy, the place your mind drifts to when life seems unbearable or you think of your heart's desires. Travel, sex, wealth, security, power, all yours for the asking. The price? Bowing down before an idol, falling down to worship the prince of lies.

Satan knows we are created for worship, knows we long to fill the void within us that only our Father can touch. Scripture (Exodus 34:12-16, Isaiah 45:23, Romans 14:11) as well as our own experiences bear this out. Since we are created to worship, if we are not in relationship to our Creator, then we will find some kind of idol—ultimately ourselves—to worship and relate to. That's why anything or anybody can so easily become an idol for us. As human beings with heart-altars intended for worship, we can easily turn in upon ourselves and resourcefully create gods that we can manage—food, sexual pleasure, our spouse, children, friends, money, our careers, hobbies, even religion can become a kind of false idol, a legalism where we feel good about ourselves because we pharisaically follow all the rules. Even in the midst of wandering in the desert, the children of Israel fashioned a golden calf to worship rather than patiently trusting and waiting on the Lord.

Jesus countered Satan the third time with the simple truth that it is God and God alone whom we are to worship and serve. If you're like me, my first thought is, "Easy for Jesus to say!" After all, of course the Son of God knows the Father so intimately that He's able to denounce idolatry and focus on glorifying His Father. But you and I, well, we still have a ways to go. This is where, I believe, we must realize and identify more fully with Christ's identity as a human being, while respectfully recognizing His full deity as God's Son. Christ remembers who He is, what He's created for, and where He's going. We are called to do the same.

2. How does Jesus' experience in the desert illustrate what it means to "struggle well"?
3. What do you think it looks like for you to struggle well? When have you experienced it?

STRUGGLING WITHOUT YIELDING

So often Christians today pretend that temptation always comes with a warning flare to point it out, as if it were a traffic accident, and consequently allowing them to avoid it. More often than not, opportunities for sin will consistently present themselves every moment of our lives. By pretending we can spot temptations a mile away, we attempt to reduce our fear that we could ever give in to them. However, such a fear would force us to depend on God more, force us to suffer and struggle more, as opposed to quickly labeling an approaching thought as "lust" (or whatever S-I-N) and running away to our "formula" for combatting it. Usually though, this amounts to nothing more than busywork. Our struggle with sin is still going to be there and the more we attempt to deny it, the more power we give it. Ironically enough, it becomes that much more tempting, like the dieter who suddenly senses every morsel of food within a ten-block radius.

Because of the Fall, we crave sin by nature. To deny this is true is to live outside the ultimate reality of God's truth. While this is not all that defines us, thanks to God's sacrificial gift of Christ, it is a reality we must accept before grace has any meaning at all. Diamonds sparkle brightest on the jeweler's dark velvet cloth; the light of grace is most illuminating in the utter darkness of our sinful hearts.

To avoid the pain of seeing our sin for what it is, Christians often cheapen grace. We become legalists, managers with well-disciplined DayTimers that don't leave room for temptation and sin. How sad and untrue! This in itself is a kind of prideful self-deception, pretending we are better than we are.

So should we just grit our teeth and endure temptations? Are there other ways to get through them? Basically, we are called to suffer temptations, to endure them without yielding to them.

Suffering temptations will look different on each of us. Always, though, it should mean running to the Father and His love, mercy, and truth about who we are and who He is. *Temptations are opportunities for spiritual reality checks that remind us of our dependence on our Abba.* This will likely mean experiencing emotions that are unpleasant, painful, unruly. Suffering temptations might mean asking other people for help, for prayer, for insight.

For a better picture still of what it means to suffer temptations without yielding to them, let's reconsider our two portraits of temptation: Adam and Eve's, and Christ's. In both scenes, Satan revels in undermining God's goodness (this strategy is blatant with Eve and implicit with Jesus) and planting self-important questions in his temptee's minds. Eve immediately latches on to the questions and the doubt of God they lead to. The serpent's line of reasoning seems reasonable enough, but its entire case presumes God is not trustworthy. It's like a geometric proof that looks sound enough, but when you examine it, you realize it assumes a right angle is a hundred degrees, not ninety.

Thomas à Kempis describes the process of yielding to temptation like this:

> First, the thought is allowed to enter into our minds.
> Second, the imagination is sparked by the thought.
> Third, we feel a sense of pleasure at the fantasy, and we
> entertain it. Fourth and finally, we engage in the evil
> action, assenting to its urges. This is how, little by little,
> temptations gain entrance and overcome us if they are
> not resisted at the beginning.[3]

Jesus, on the other hand, does not even allow temptation to take root in His mind. He sees through Satan's "proof" immediately and reminds Himself and Satan of God's goodness, sovereignty, and mercy. Eve relies on her own logic, trusting her own judgment.

TEMPTATION FROM GOD-GIVEN LONGINGS

Interestingly enough, Eve's three criteria for deciding whether to eat the fruit are basically the same three areas of temptation that Satan uses to strike at Christ: the physical (hunger), self-identity, and power (the desire for purpose). Could it be that there's something inherent and even good about these three areas of longing within us?

While resisting temptations requires choosing to trust God and exercise faith in the midst of extraordinary tension, too often I believe we throw out the baby with the bath water by labeling all longings and desires as selfish, sinful, "flesh"-generated, and depraved. We must acknowledge that if we have been redeemed and are in the life-process of sanctification through Christ, then our Father also redeems our longings and desires. In fact, so many of those heart longings were placed there by God in the first place and perverted by our sinful nature, not created by it. While it's easier to recognize that physical desires are not bad in themselves (God gave us bodies that require nourishment, sexuality as an expression of Himself and for procreation, etc.), we must also realize that He created us to have identity and purpose through Him. *In light of this, it's extremely important to be aware when you struggle with temptation so that you can identify what about it appeals to you.*

Let's look at an example by returning to Steve, our workaholic husband and father who's struggling with pornography. Recall your reaction to that scenario. It might go something like this: "Well, I know pornography is wrong, certainly a perversion of what God intended for our sexuality. If Steve is a Christian, surely he knows this, too. So why doesn't he fight the temptation? Why doesn't he simply pray, memorize Scripture, join an accountability group, or get counseling?"

Or perhaps your response to Steve's situation was more like this: "I don't struggle with pornography, but I sure know what it's like to struggle with loneliness, fear, being overwhelmed by job pressures, missing my spouse, longing for friends, wanting friends who care about me. I find myself saying and doing things that I know hurt deeply the ones I love most. I wonder what would help Steve or me or any of us to resist temptations, struggle well, and exercise our faith?"

If the first response runs the risk of being oversimplified and legalistic (by assuming a "formula" or "fix-it" can take care of Steve's problem), then the second response risks the extreme of identifying with another's struggle and then simply resigning ourselves to temptation as unconquerable just because it's inevitable.

However, notice that in both responses, the goal is on helping to eliminate the temptation, rather than seeing how the temptation might lead Steve closer to trusting God. The exercise of faith required to overcome temptation is not some isolated, lonely, passionless endeavor, but rather a re-connection with our Father who loves us, a reminder of His character, love, and grace. *Bottom line, every temptation is an opportunity to choose to worship God.*

Examining our temptations and trying to sort through our true heart longings versus the perversion of those longings can point us back to God. For Steve this might mean a painful and confusing examination of himself, his loneliness, his marriage, and his faith. In other words, the fact that he struggles with pornography is only symptomatic of much greater problems, fears, and struggles. It's not so much that he's irresistibly drawn to the glossy pages of a magazine over the loving touch of his wife; it's something much deeper. He, like all of us, presently yearns for Heaven, the ultimate hope of our future reality. This hunger is so ravenous in certain moments—especially moments of pain, struggle, or uncontrollable circumstances—that we often yield to any temptation rather than suffer through those feelings.

While many factors come into play in any struggle, part of the problem is indeed Steve's sinfulness, and how this spills over into the way he handles his loneliness, his marriage, and his way of relating to others. He refuses to take initiative (notice how he passively accepts his busyness and his wife's unavailability), communicate (he second-guesses that his friends are too busy for him), or suffer (rather than face his feelings, he "instinctively" heads for pornography).

However, we must not overlook the fact that Steve makes choices here. As we've seen, God's gift of free will carries with it the responsibility to choose. While Steve's flight to pornography feels "natural" (because he's inherently selfish as we all are, and because he can justify his behavior on the grounds of loneliness, an absent wife, and lack of friends), it is a form of idolatry, ultimately, self-idolatry.

God will not immediately alleviate our pain in this fallen world or rescue us from the consequences of our sin and others' sin. But rather than trusting Him and willingly suffering the present ache, we quickly find ways to feel better, to remove the source of our discomfort, even to retaliate at those who hurt us most. The combination of our free will with our inherent selfishness often forges a deep commitment in us to make our lives work without needing God.

Scripture consistently presents this rebellion as idolatry.

"For My people have committed two evils:
They have forsaken Me,

The fountain of living waters,
To hew for themselves cisterns,
Broken cisterns,
That can hold no water." (Jeremiah 2:13)

This self-sufficient, rebellious inclination is perhaps the core button Satan tries to push with us. He knows we're inclined to trust ourselves more than God and His will for us. This selfishness combined with the fact that we are all created to worship, and will in fact find something to worship in order to survive, allows Satan to simply reinforce our inclination toward idolatry with whatever bait is at hand. We all want to find something that feels like life to us and that we can control: the affirmation of others; pleasure in the form of food, sex, shopping, or numerous other addictions; self-protection from the inherent painfulness of life and relationship with others.

EMBRACING TEMPTATIONS

So is there a place for embracing temptations, for facing them head-on despite the fear that we might succumb to them? Yes. As I mentioned before, we are pridefully arrogant to pretend that we can avoid them altogether. Temptations are an inherent part of the tension between our fallen nature (which continues to die) and our new redeemed nature (which continues to grow).

We should keep in mind, however, that God's grace should never be used as license to give in to temptations (Romans 6:15). Rather, God desires us to view temptations as opportunities to trust Him, to exercise faith in Him and not in our own judgments and abilities, even if it feels crazy and irrational to do so. In this respect, embracing temptations in order to know and love our Father at a deeper, richer, more passionate level is an integral part of the repentance process. Instead of working so hard to rid ourselves of temptation (and alleviating ourselves of their painful tensions), we need to take the focus off ourselves and the discomfort temptations produce, and instead view them as a time to worship, even when we don't feel like it.

For instance, Steve might examine and face his loneliness and prayerfully cry out to God about what he feels. This kind of lament is not grumbling self-pity, but rather an honest heart-cry that seeks God despite the pain of present circumstances. From this point he might call his wife and share his pain with her, or he might call her up and seek to lovingly minister to her loneliness rather than staying fixated on his own. He might call up friends and schedule a lunch for whenever they are available. He might be vulnerable enough to tell his friends he misses them, needs their prayers, and is struggling.

Michelle, similarly, might face her fears and other painful emotions, her fears of failure in her marriage, motherhood, and relationship with God. She might spend time in solitude, in Scripture, in spending time with her husband or other friends rather than actively seeking busywork to occupy her time.

Facing and embracing temptations as an opportunity to trust the Father deeper is the picture Christ exemplifies as He struggles in the desert. He holds steadfastly to His Father as His life, refusing to allow His physical hunger, His human desire for identity and self-awareness, and His desire for purpose to interfere. By trusting His Father for what He most desires, Christ practices faith in His Father's character and goodness. He knows that because of the Father's love and goodness, He has identity, purpose, and physical life.

When we trust the Father in the same way, we can view temptations as inevitable, yet not the focus of our faith journeys. They can be conquered and take us to new levels of trust and faith in God. And even when we fail, temptations can still become incredible occasions for tasting our Lord's grace, the Abba Father who runs down the road to warmly embrace and forgive His prodigal children.

The other important point to keep in mind, and from which to draw much comfort and hope, is the gift of the Holy Spirit. I believe the Spirit is the major presence who offers us the means of escaping and overcoming temptation that Paul refers to in 1 Corinthians 10:13. The Spirit urges us to remember what is true, the spiritual realities of God's character and our new life in Him, rather than give in to the fleeting pleasure of lies. As we saw in chapter 1 and will hear echoed throughout this book, the entire process of repentance involves our desire to turn toward God and away from self. While impossible through our own striving, we are aided and empowered by the Holy Spirit, the life-giver indwelling our hearts and guiding us toward the will of our unsurpassably loving Father.

JOURNALING THE JOURNEY

As I look back over my journal entries, I see the struggle with temptation reflected time and time again. Should I or shouldn't I? What if I don't know what the "right" decision is? What if I can't always see the means of escape from a temptation that God provides? As you can see, these are just a few of my own recurring questions in the midst of temptations with lust, envy, hatred, overeating, jealousy, and self-protection.

From My Journal

I did it again. Christmas is still two weeks away and I've already overspent what I budgeted for presents. And maybe that's not such a big deal, but when I think about why I overspent, why I kept thinking of more and more people I should buy presents for, that's where it gets scary. I want people to like me. I want them to feel loved and appreciated by me. No, if I'm truly honest, I want them indebted to me, obligated to care about me or grant me a favor.

Feels like the temptation to overspend is just the tip of the iceberg. Amid all the hustle and bustle of shopping, Christmas parties with friends and coworkers, and family activities, I feel lost. I want some kind of connection with God, but it's so much easier to withdraw, fantasize, or have another slice of fruitcake. I think to wrestle with these issues means finding some quiet moments, making some unpopular decisions and saying no to some fun invitations, taking more of a firm leadership of our

*family's Christmas time. Things I don't particularly like. Espe-
cially when it's so much easier to just go with the flow and keep
singing "Jingle Bells" with a fake smile plastered on my face. But
I want more than that. I want God more than that.*

For Your Journal

What do you consider your greatest temptation, the most frustrating sinful habit that you repeatedly battle? How often do you
confront it? Describe your last struggle with it. Who would you
be if you didn't have this struggle?

Consider the following Scripture from one of Paul's letters:

Now that we know what we have—Jesus, this great High
Priest with ready access to God—let's not let it slip
through our fingers. We don't have a priest who is out of
touch with our reality. He's been through weakness and
testing, experienced it all—all but the sin. So let's walk
right up to him and get what he is so ready to give. Take
the mercy, accept the help. (Hebrews 4:15-16, MESSAGE)

How would you define the help and mercy mentioned here? Can
you think of times you've experienced it? How could you appropriate them more in the midst of temptations? How do you feel
about the prospect of living a life filled with temptations without losing hope?

3

ADDICTIONS

As I sit here writing this chapter in my basement office at home, I'm well into my fourth cup of coffee and it's only 7:00 a.m. (That explains a lot, you're saying to yourself!) I would agree that I rely on caffeine too heavily to give me that extra boost that gets me going in the morning and sustains me throughout the day. Should I give it up? Is it sinful? Is it an addiction? Are all addictions sinful? Some more than others?

Perhaps you have certain sinful habits that you can't shake no matter how hard you try. Patterns that you feel stuck in, that you always give in to, that seem to go far beyond the mere temptations we discussed in the last chapter. They may run the spectrum of virtually all human behaviors. Maybe you love to shop and can't resist a great sale, a unique pair of designer shoes, or the latest CD. Or it could be you feel bound to alcohol, tobacco, prescription medication, chocolate, illegal drugs, masturbation, gossip, gambling, or a host of other activities or substances. In fact, we probably all have repetitive behaviors we wish we didn't.

Addictions obviously hinder the repentance process, but

why? What's the source of their powerful hold on our lives? And better yet, can we break free from the tight grip they seem to hold on us? What does breaking free from addictions cost us? These are important questions that we will discuss throughout this chapter, but first let's consider how we're even going to define *addiction*.

---

1. What do you think of when you hear the word *addiction*? What shapes your definition? How have addictions affected your life to this point?

WHAT IS ADDICTION?

While *addiction* has become a pop psych buzzword in our culture, it is not a new concept. In fact, many of the mystics (a term applied to a group of medieval Christian believers who actively pursued the mystery of knowing God through Christ and often wrote about their experiences) used the word *attachment*—from the old French *attaché*, meaning "nailed to"[1]—to refer to the powerful attraction various sins hold for each of us.

On the other hand, psychologists and doctors typically define an addiction as any compulsive, habitual reliance on a behavior or substance. The term first emerged from the physical dependence experienced by narcotics users and alcoholics. Physiologically, our bodies can become hooked by addictive substances that provide pleasure or relief to the body and brain. A pattern is created neurologically in which we "remember" the pleasurable effect of the substance or behavior and crave it. If we don't get our addictive object we experience withdrawal symptoms—anxiety, depression, anger, stress, nausea, headaches, etc. The other chief physiological effect of any addiction is tolerance, the increasing need for the desired substance or behavior in order to produce the pleasurable relief. In the past few decades, doctors have documented that people can become psychologically addicted to things that have no physically addictive properties. In other words, if we come to rely on something or someone immoderately and consistently to bring us pleasure, relief from the pain of life, or revenge at people and God for not coming through for us, then we are addicted.

WHY DO WE BECOME ADDICTED?

As you can see, the external description of an addiction is something we can usually all agree on, Christians and nonChristians alike. The key point of divergence, however, is likely more important, at least for our purposes. Why do people do what they do? What is the basis for the addiction, the motivation? Two primary reasons emerge: (1) *the influence of past experiences and conditioning,* and (2) *the present gratification it provides*. Let's consider the former reason first.

Past Experience

Scripture gives us many examples of the way we are often shaped by our surrounding environment. The Proverbs resound with such truths as,

> Train up a child in the way he should go,
> Even when he is old he will not depart from it. (22:6)

The Apostle Paul had been trained to hate Christians; Timothy was brought up to love and serve the Lord. While modern psychology might claim to have "discovered" this truth that our surroundings shape our identities and world views, they have actually just uncovered the truth of God's Word. It seems logical and verifiable that what we see, hear, and feel every day shapes how we think about ourselves, God, and the world, and consequently who we become, what we envision.

But while psychology typically stops with past history and behavioral conditioning for causation, as Christians we know we are not bound by our abilities, pasts, parents, etc. Certainly our pasts and conditioning affect us tremendously, but they do not solely define us. God loves us far too much to abandon us to what we can accomplish in ourselves; yet, while He pursues us relentlessly, He also gives us the free will to choose to accept

Him or not. Thus, we are not bound by our pasts and the conditioning they may have instilled in us. We may still be affected by the past, and likely will be, but we are not imprisoned by it. God offers us new life in Christ, change through the process of spiritual transformation, and the hope of Heaven through His goodness and mercy.

Paul was not condemned to his bitter, obsessive quest to kill Christians and annihilate God's Word. Jesus dramatically intervened and offered him life, including the change that loving and serving God brings. Jesus extends this same invitation to all of us, to leave behind our old selves and embrace His salvation.

> And such were some of you [fornicators, idolators, adulterers, homosexuals, thieves, covetous, drunkards, revilers, and swindlers]; but you were washed, but you were sanctified, but you were justified in the name of the Lord Jesus Christ, and in the Spirit of our God.
> (1 Corinthians 6:11)

Or perhaps you grew up in a Christian home and were trained in godly ways. Nonetheless, you are still susceptible to addictions, basically because we are all susceptible to the attraction of sin.

Present Gratification

The present gratification of addictions is, likewise, not something newly recognized by doctors and therapists. Scripture expounds on the temptations of the flesh, the temporary pleasure that yielding to sin produces. (Check out Proverbs 1:10-15, 5:3, and 7:6-21—notice the way the adulteress represents sin with all her seductive pleasures of the moment.) If sin were not so appealing, if it didn't satisfy a desire (some legitimate, some perverted) at some level in us, then it would not be difficult to resist. However, the fact that we remain mortals in a fallen world reminds us that we are always looking for ways to feel pleasure and comfort and eliminate (or at least alleviate) pain and other "negative" emotions.

FALSE WORSHIP: THE PARADOX OF ADDICTIONS

So if we're all affected, directly and indirectly, by our selfish, addictive natures, how do we live with them without resigning ourselves to them? Do we simply try harder? How much of the power of addictions can be controlled and changed through sheer willpower and behavior modification?

A good deal, if the current trends in counseling and psychology are any indication. Terms such as *recovery*, *Twelve Steps*, *inner child*, and even *addiction* itself all testify to our culture's fascination with self-discovery and improvement. While God certainly can and does use a multitude of channels for His glory and grace, including the recovery movement and much of popular psychology, there is a fundamental flaw in its understanding and approach to humankind.

The recovery movement typically does not acknowledge our need for God through Christ. Thus, the goal becomes self-focused—recovering our inner child, healing our past wounds, confronting and/or blaming our parents or whomever has harmed us. Recovery movement followers assert that self-awareness, higher self-esteem, and control over our lives can change us into happy, healthy, well-adjusted adults.

While there are certainly seeds of truth here, the focus is terribly skewed. As Christians we come back to a different foundation about who we are and what we need. Our identity is not in ourselves, the dysfunctional family we were born into, or the behavior patterns we can trace. Rather, we are image-bearers of our Creator Father, born with sinful natures as a consequence of our ultimate parents in the garden. We are created to worship, to be in relationship with God, to know, love, and glorify Him, not ourselves.

A quick review of chapter 2 reminds us that so much of the serpent's strategy in tempting Eve and Adam appealed to their desire to change this fundamental truth about their identities. "You could be like God if you eat this apple." And think through this deceptive formula for a moment. We can be like God; we can have power and wisdom and goodness in and of ourselves.

And if we're like Him, we don't really need Him, do we? If we can be deceived or deceive ourselves into believing that we're not so bad, or that we can make up for any badness in us by doing good (a merit system), then we function as our own idol. We falsely believe we can determine ultimate reality rather than seeing our mortal limits and viewing the more eternal perspective of God's divine tapestry-drama in which we are but one player, not the star around which the whole play revolves.

Ironically, though, we come to rely not just on ourselves but on something outside ourselves, the "apple" of our addictions, to provide the catalyst for self-worship. And this is where addictions, and false idols, serve two important functions in the worship process. One, *they make us feel powerful in our ability to "control" the behavior or object;* we can have it at our own convenience, any time things are not going our way. Two, *they make us feel good by taking us out of ourselves, out of the pain, discomfort, anger, or unpleasant feelings that real life in a fallen world inevitably brings.* So this counterfeit worship allows us to touch the fringe of our real identities and longings while falsely believing we're in control.

True worship, on the other hand, humbles us by our neediness and dependence on the Father and calls us to face the painful reality of our sinful world while still being part of God's bigger plan. True worship leaves us with a uniquely personal glimpse of our Father and a deeper yearning for the eternal worship that Heaven will bring.

Our struggler Steve might help flesh out this picture. In the scenario presented last chapter, Steve chose to return to pornography rather than face his loneliness which could lead him to God. What he most longs for—true intimacy with One greater than himself, a sense of purpose that will motivate him to suffer, connection to others like his wife and friends—can never take place when he chooses the idolatry of sexual fantasies. In fact, he only increases his loneliness; after the few minutes of pleasure, the deep yearning within is still present, a bit numbed perhaps, but still there.

On the other hand, if Steve had chosen to face his loneliness, the empty feeling inside, the longing for his wife, for other brothers, he would be forced to cry out to God. Like the psalmist and Christ he might cry out, "My God, my God, why have you forsaken me? Why do I feel so alone?" (Psalm 22:1). This would force Steve to admit that he does indeed long to sense God's presence, to feel His comforting embrace, to want God more than to be taken out of his loneliness. Oddly enough, such a lament, full of the pain of perceived abandonment and the fear of doubt, creates a place where God can indeed speak to us, hold us, love us.

> 2. How does the fact that we're created to worship open us up to the power of addictions? Can you identify with this situation?

So how do we overcome addictions? Do we have to overcome them as evidence of God's presence in our lives? How much of this process is His job and how much is ours?

Again, I believe we must realize that overcoming addictions is not God's main priority for our lives. Certainly He's concerned with them because we're often using them to worship idols rather than Him, the one true God, and He is a jealous God. However, my bet is that God is not nearly as concerned about the behavioral aspects of addictive behavior as He is about what it does to our relationship with Him, what it does to our hearts and our reflection of Him.

THE CHOICE TO SUFFER

Like so much of our fallen nature and fallen world, our addictions are another opportunity for God's redemptive power to manifest itself. Unfortunately, many of us often want God simply to intervene and deliver us from the addictive behavior because it's uncomfortably painful, not because we desire Him more. We want Him to be a problem-solver, a kind of magic genie, who can take away our pain simply because we want Him to. However, God will not be used or controlled in this way. He much prefers to use our proclivity for addiction as a means to reveal our deep longing to worship and love Him.

And perhaps you're saying that's what you desire as well. So what's the problem then? Why do our addictions remain such a thorny barrier between us and God? While all of us have the same offer of life through Christ extended to us, and many have accepted it, we still cling to our endeavors for change rather than seeking God. The old behaviors still haunt us long after we've accepted Christ, grown in the Word, and found a community of faithful believers. The result is that we believe our relationship with God can only do so much toward changing us into the kind of people we'd rather be. And if we trace this to the foundation of its false logic, we either believe that God's grace is not enough for us (maybe for others) or that God's way is not our way (it's too hard). And so we choose at some level to continue just getting by. We want to know God, we want to love others with grace and passion, but we also feel bound to sin, to addictions, to the objects, people, or substances that paradoxically both relieve us and keep us from what we really want.

So what keeps us from simply being obedient? We know gossiping, sexual immorality, and stealing are wrong; we know Christ heals our hearts through forgiveness and salvation. What then keeps us going back again and again until a sinful habit is so entrenched in our hearts that it feels like it has a life of its own? *Much of it has to do with whether or not we choose to suffer in order to know our Father* or whether we choose to try to take ourselves out of the immediate pain, doubt, or fear. When we consistently refuse to take the risk to act on faith, to be obedient even though it doesn't feel as good as masturbating or overeating or gossiping, then larger faith issues feel even more impossible. But obedience must arise out of a passion to know the Father, to believe His love is true and abiding, His presence real and genuine in our lives, even when we can't feel it. We must make small, everyday choices in order to see our faith grow, and our repentant hearts stretched.

Steve, our struggler who feels addicted to pornography, might express his struggle this way: "Being faithful in the small things—like resisting daily temptations—feels so futile. As long as I can keep my sin hidden from my family and pretend there are no consequences, why not give in to temptation?" By refusing to even fight temptation, Steve also refuses to hope in things presently unseen. In other words, he refuses to act on faith, the hope that God does love and care about him and his needs and desires. The instant gratification of self often blinds us, like Steve, to the desire we have of hoping in God. This hope usually requires that we wait patiently, that we suffer with the addictive cravings for relief, in light of a deeper longing for the only God who satisfies our souls. True faith requires us to fight the good fight, even though we may fail sometimes, in order to hope more deeply in our Father and to long more fully for relationship with Him.

Addictions, on the other hand, resign us to defeat without much of a struggle at all. We want to feel something, to worship and feel good about ourselves and have something give our life some meaning, but we balk at waiting on God, at suffering the temporary for the eternal. It's like knowing we're sick and knowing that we desire to be well, but choosing to take just enough medicine to knock the edge off our disease. We want life on our own terms, not God's, and we typically pay for this ambivalence by living mediocre lives.

"DO YOU WANT TO GET WELL?"

However, Christ enters our lives and hearts to forever shatter this binding of the human heart. As was often the case in His ministry, Christ healed souls, not just imperfect bodies. In the following encounter, notice the question Christ uses as a focal point.

> Now there is in Jerusalem by the Sheep Gate a pool, which in Aramaic is called Betheseda and which is surrounded by five covered colonnades. Here a great

number of disabled people used to lie—the blind, the lame, the paralyzed. One who was there had been an invalid for thirty-eight years. When Jesus saw him lying there and learned that he had been in this condition for a long time, he asked him, "Do you want to get well?"

"Sir," the invalid replied, "I have no one to help me into the pool when the water is stirred. While I am trying to get in, someone else goes down ahead of me."

Then Jesus said to him, "Get up! Pick up your mat and walk." At once the man was cured; he picked up his mat and walked. (John 5:2-9, NIV)

Let's pause for a moment before continuing with the rest of the story. First, I realize that being afflicted with physical infirmities is not the same thing as being addicted to crack cocaine, chocolate, or gossip about the pastor's wife. However, I believe an analogy can be made without compromising the integrity of this passage. It's important to note, though, that by making this analogy, I am in no way trying to support the definition of an addiction as merely a disease that simply descends upon us without our involvement.

As with many physical diseases, it's often our small choices which lead to graver consequences. While we might not choose to have the flu, we will choose to stay up late, overwork ourselves, and let our bodies become run-down from lack of rest. When asked if we want cancer, we'd respond with a resounding "No!" but this doesn't keep some of us from smoking.

My point is this: Addictive behavior usually ends up with us feeling powerless over the desired object, but our powerlessness did not happen overnight. And even when we feel powerless, we still have choices. Alcoholics and others may even be genetically predisposed to the power of certain addictions, but this must not be passively accepted as a disease that, at best, lies dormant, waiting to strike at any opportunity. We make choices out of our free wills, including addictive as well as holy choices.

Returning to our passage, notice that Jesus respects the free will of the lame man. Why in the world would Christ ask the man, "Do you want to get well?" when Jesus knew the man's history—his thirty-eight-year bout with crippling affliction? It might even seem cruel if you or I were to ask a paraplegic, "Do you wish you could walk?" But if we trust the perfect, loving character of Christ, then why did He ask the man? Why not simply proceed to healing him?

Perhaps it has something to do with Jesus' knowledge of human nature. Perhaps He understands about our selfish, idolatrous, addictive natures, about the way we stutter-step down the path of faith, two steps forward, one step back. We want to trust Him, to love and glorify Him, but only as far as we can see, not around the dark, foggy bends in the road that living a life of faith requires. So, perhaps, Christ's question, "Do you want to get well?" reflects the same gift of free will that the Father placed in Adam and Eve.

Examine your heart honestly for a moment. Do you want to be well? Do you want the wholeness of being the man or woman your Father created you to be? Do you desire Him above all else, knowing the cost to be beyond comprehension and yet to be the most free gift of all? How do you answer our Lord's question based on the way you live your life? *Do you want to get well so long as it doesn't hurt, or are you willing to know the fullness of His healing by paradoxically taking your eyes off your own pain?*

The lame man at the pool of Bethesda does not respond to Christ's question with cynicism, bitterness, or incredulity. In his mind, his healing is contingent on getting in the pool first, and since he has no one to help him, others always beat him to the healing waters. He responds to the inquiring stranger, probably hoping for a strong set of arms to lift him into the pool. Out of his earnestness, his indirect reply to Jesus' question, comes his choice. Yes, he does wish to be well. Our Lord speaks and he is healed; the man lifts his ragged pallet and walks for the first time in thirty-eight years, a feat others might have deemed impossible. But this man chose faith.

THE COST OF WELLNESS

The story continues as the healing becomes a focal point for the legalistic Jews about the rules of the Sabbath, and ultimately about the identity and authority of the Messiah. The cured man tells the Jewish leaders of his healing and the stranger's gentle command to "Pick up your mat and walk." After this, Jesus seeks out the healed man in the temple and says, "See, you are well again. Stop sinning or something worse may happen to you." The healed man then "went away and told the Jews that it was Jesus who had made him well" (John 5:14-15, NIV).

What are we to make of this part of the story? How does it fit in with desiring God more than desiring the object of our addictions? This last half of the story raises at least two important complications. One is Jesus' deliberate (He seeks the man out) message concerning what is true about the healed man's new status. The other is the healed man's response to this message.

It's almost as if Jesus knows the man is not fully aware of what has taken place, of what the life-changing implications are, in his healing. Jesus begins by pointing out the obvious but unfathomable—you're healed, you've been made well. While the man along with the Jewish religious leaders can see that the man is well by the fact that he's walking around, they do not necessarily or readily embrace the reality of it. They do not want to examine the implications, because that intrudes into their lives, requiring other choices, less self-centered, less manageable choices, regarding the way they relate to God and live their lives.

How often do we embrace our status as redeemed people, children of our heavenly King, but balk at what He asks of us? We want the privileges, the status, we want redemption, but we want it without cost or suffering, without having to walk the stony path of faith, without working out our salvation with fear and trembling. We accept the free gift of salvation through Christ but resist living out of it. The focus remains on ourselves and not the God we ultimately desire to serve and glorify.

After pointing out the obvious but not-so-obvious truth about the man's condition, Jesus instructs, perhaps, even warns, the man, "Stop sinning or something worse may happen to you" (5:14). What does this mean? Surely Christ didn't expect the man to be sin-free, to have a divine nature just because his body is cured. No, I believe Christ refers to His first question to the man. In the sense that His question, "Do you want to be well?" addresses the man's will, so does His admonition concerning sin. In other words, don't choose sin, don't seek it out, don't live a life centered on self. And what should we make of the warning "or something worse may happen to you"? Does this mean that if the man returns to sinning he will become lame again? We don't know, and more importantly, his lameness becomes secondary to his soul, to his choice to live a life pursuing God or self.

This passage is sometimes used to reinforce the consequences of the "unpardonable sin" of blaspheming against the Spirit described in Matthew 12:30-32. This concept certainly raises numerous issues of interpretation. Without going into all of them, I contend that the general meaning of Christ's warning is evident from the context of the passage. The "something worse" contrasts with the man's previous condition of being lame for thirty-eight years. The implication is that to return to sinning, to refuse to live out of an encounter with the Messiah, yields far worse eternal consequences than the temporary physical affliction the man previously knew.

Perhaps the implication for us is that the things we make so important, the horrible, sobering, painful, excruciating events— childhood abuse, rape, the death of loved ones, the ravages of disease, loneliness, abandonment—are not nearly as important as they feel to us in the present moment. The effects of such events are immediately painful and uncontrollable and we perceive them as overwhelming and unbearable. However, as tangible, immediate, and horrible as they may be, they still pale in comparison to what ultimately matters, our relationship with God. Once again, we come back to our simple and profound description of true repentance: turning toward God in the middle of every circumstance.

So does this passage imply that we can lose our salvation if we keep sinning after we have accepted Christ? I do not believe so. At least, I don't believe Christ's admonition to "stop sinning" refers to the kind of sinning that is inherently part of the struggle of life, that tension we discussed between our old sinful nature and our new redeemed heart. I believe instead it refers to our ultimate heart attitude, that if we did indeed choose God's gift of grace through His Son's sacrifice as a means to know and love Him, we will not lose our desire for Him despite how big we may blow it. If on the other hand, we've merely been playing games all along, accepting Christ as a plea-bargain to get what we want out of life, seeking God as an answer to our problems rather than using them as a pathway to know Him, then I think our situation is far worse than mere illness. If one is fully aware of who Christ is and the message of grace He brings, and still chooses self (or any other idol) over Him, then I believe God becomes limited by virtue of His gift of free will to us. He will not impose Himself where He is not wanted or invited. If we love ourselves more than we desire to love Him, He will let us.

Perhaps you disagree. But even if your theology differs, I believe most of us would agree that God desires our hearts in relationship with Him, that He is more concerned with our eternal well-being and not just the immediate gratification we are so attuned to. With this in mind then, ask yourself, "Do I want to be well? Am I aware of how much I ultimately desire God more than any of these other silly things I so quickly turn my heart toward?"

3. Put yourself in the lame man's place. What kind of healing is needed in your life? What would it look like for you to pick up your mat and walk again?

4. Why is it "far worse" for us to encounter the healing truth of the gospel and still choose sinfulness over faithfulness?

THE PATH TOWARD HOME

In our day when blame-shifting is expected and commonplace, I believe the temptation for us is simply to dilute our sins into addictions. And, of course, if they're addictions, then they're caused by unmet needs for parental affirmation from childhood, fear of intimacy, or lack of self-esteem. So as long as we can "explain" why certain addictions (sinful habits) plague us, then we don't have to own them, feel the weight of them, see the damage they do to others, acknowledge their unacceptability to God. We're off the hook.

But this must not be the case! While we must certainly acknowledge that addictions, both physical and psychological, have serious and tangible effects, we cannot use this as a scapegoat. If we're using the addictions label to justify sinful behavior and excuse ourselves, then we've gotten off the path of seeking God. "What then? Shall we sin because we are not under law but under grace? May it never be!" (Romans 6:15). If we too readily embrace the fact of our addictive natures as a way to avoid the truth about who we are and what we're created for, then God becomes no more important or powerful to us than our weekly counseling session or the latest self-help book.

So how do we acknowledge addictions as a barrier to knowing God without slipping into self-absorption and justification? We remind ourselves once more of who we are and who God is. We must remember that we always have choices. When we surrender our power to choose, the basis of our will, whether to another person, a bottle of vodka, or the malicious whispers of the gossip's tongue, then we sacrifice the freedom that comes from loving our Father first. We must embrace the struggle of temptations and addictions as a pathway to our truest desires to love and know our Abba Father, rather than an internal cue to control our lives with cheap counterfeits.

By remembering who God is, we are also reminded of our desire to worship and serve Him. We recall His character, the ways He has mercifully loved, provided, and pursued us even in the deserts and storms of life. We count the blessings and monuments to His faithfulness that point us to His goodness and grace once more. Certainly this is bound to be painful. While peace and joy may be felt, a certain level of suffering will also be required since we are not yet in Heaven, face to face with our Father. If we allow our addictions to remind us of our longings and of who God is, we will suffer the same depth of sorrow and grief that Adam and Eve experienced after the Fall. We will long for the glorious completion of our identities in Christ, for the unsurpassable joy of intimacy with our Father, for the rest and energy permeating our eternal home.

Indeed, this is where our self-absorbed, selfish, addictive natures can lead us to our knees before our loving Father. Like the prodigal who wakes up in the pigpen aware that there's so much more with even the least of what his father offers, aware of his grievous sin against his father, we come to our senses. Our inclinations toward addictions become a persistent reminder of our capacity to worship, our need for the love of God.

Paradoxically, in our attempts to master our own destinies by finding outlets of relief, pleasure, and control we become enslaved to our addictions. We realize that even in our selfish attempts to control our own worlds, we do not have the power to resist the very objects that we hoped gave us the power over our lives in the first place. This is confusing, perhaps, but profoundly hopeful. For in the despair of realizing our addictive natures, we are humbled and reminded once more of our need for God.

In his book *Addiction and Grace*, Gerald May describes the paradox this way:

> We may go through a great deal of humbling, if not outright humiliation, before we come to this simplicity of hope. We do not like admitting defeat, and we will struggle valiantly, even foolishly, to prove we can master our destinies. God, in whose image we are made, instills in us the capacity for relentless tenacity, an assertiveness that complements our yearning hunger for God. But most of us overdo it; our spirit of assertiveness quickly

becomes a spirit of pride. We will never really turn to God in loving openness as long as we are handling things well enough by ourselves. And it is precisely our most powerful addictions that cause us to defeat ourselves, that bring us to the rock bottom realization that we cannot finally master everything. Thus, although in one sense addiction is the enemy of grace, it can also be a powerful channel for the flow of grace.[2]

This powerful channel, which we often condemn as weakness and powerlessness, can lead us back to God. In fact, the very process of redemptive repentance becomes opportunity for us to know God in fresh, more intimate ways. We become more aware of our fundamental need for Him, for His forgiveness, mercy, and love. As Oswald Chambers puts it, "Once we see ourselves under the canopy of God's overflowing mercy we are dissolved in wonder, love and praise. That is the meaning of repentance, which is the greatest gift God ever gives a man."[3]

Finally, we are reminded by the Apostle Paul of the power our weaknesses and struggles have to draw us to the Father. Even this great saint, the evangelist to the Gentiles, struggled with "a thorn in the flesh," which he prayed to be taken away. What he received instead comforts and inspires us all:

Because of the extravagance of those revelations, and so I wouldn't get a big head, I was given the gift of a handicap to keep me in constant touch with my limitations. Satan's angel did his best to get me down; what he in fact did was push me to my knees. No danger then of walking around high and mighty! At first I didn't think of it as a gift, and begged God to remove it. Three times I did that, and then he told me,

"My grace is enough; it's all you need.
My strength comes into its own in your weakness."

Once I heard that, I was glad to let it happen. I quit focusing on the handicap and began appreciating the gift.

It was a case of Christ's strength moving in on my weakness. Now I take limitations in stride, and with good cheer, these limitations that cut me down to size—abuse, accidents, opposition, bad breaks. I just let Christ take over! And so the weaker I get, the stronger I become. (2 Corinthians 12:7-10, MESSAGE)

Perhaps we have not yet reached Paul's maturity to readily view our addictions as gifts. But his perspective certainly sobers us to the reality of what is going on, a spiritual struggle. With that in mind, and without simplistically "letting go and letting God," we can embrace our weaknesses as vehicles of faith, pathways back to our heart's true desire, and reflectors of our Father's glory.

Addictions, then, are not just habits to be repented of; they reflect our very natures—the sinful depravity and the desire by design to worship. A repentant heart breaks addictions by facing the full spectrum of emotions that accompany the habit, getting help from others—a friend, spouse, or counselor—as necessary (more about community and accountability in chapter 7), and viewing the hunger underlying the addiction as a holy appetite for the one true God. A repentant heart chooses to struggle to break old, sinful habits, fails occasionally, but fights onward.

JOURNALING THE JOURNEY

From My Journal

Another new year and time to recall the unkept resolutions from last year. How many times do I try harder only to blow it time after time? I think my autobiography will be called The Billionth Beginning *or something like that. It's been a hard week, and I don't know where to go from here. I want to go forward, go up, go on, but feel stuck like I do so much of the time. The week was especially hard for two reasons: (1) finances, worrying about budgets, paying Christmas bills, etc. and (2) intense loneliness and longing for friendships. The two things I wanted in the mail yesterday say a lot—the new credit card I sent off for and a letter from my best friend back home. Neither one came.*

And I lived. I was depressed most of the day, as I have been most of the week, and I hate it. And if I'm honest, what I hate most is seeing how I use money and friendships to keep me in control of my life, to keep me afloat materially and emotionally.

I'm going to make some resolutions anyway, even though I probably won't keep them all. I will try to break them down into daily-sized bites. I will remember why I'm being obedient, what I most desire. Maybe I'll suffer more weeks like this one, view them as times to worship rather than times to overspend or have someone take me out of my discomfort. There is hope.

For Your Journal

Think about what's been going on inside you as you've read this chapter. What are the addictions in your life? Which ones frighten you the most? Which ones seem to have the most power over you?

How have you dealt with them in the past? To what end? What's your mood at this point—hopeful, discouraged, desperate, urgent, complacent?

What does it mean for you to be faithful in small choices, every day, in order to live out your heart's ultimate desire of knowing your Father?

4

THE FEELINGS OF REPENTANCE

—

As Steve pulled out of the parking lot and headed home, his heart was reeling. How could that have been him in that adult bookstore? No matter how bad it seemed at home with Anne, he still loved her and the kids. He wanted to be a good husband and father. What would they do if they ever found out about his habit? Of course, they wouldn't understand. He didn't even understand it himself.

And then there was God. What did he do with God while he browsed through this dingy building? Steve knew God still loved him and forgave him, but sometimes Steve wondered how long God would let his secret go unpunished. "God is holy and just. And I know I still love Him, that He's my father and Christ is my brother. But why does my life feel so hard, so empty? I guess I'll have to try harder to be a strong Christian," Steve thought to himself. "Maybe that will take my struggle away."

Joanne replaced the phone on its cradle and felt her whole body go numb. It wasn't someone calling with bad news, but rather a call she'd made herself. Her friend Vicki had convinced her to spread the word about seeing the pastor's wife coming out of the liquor store this week. She had felt sophomoric and catty, but also compelled to do whatever it took to stay with the in-group in her church singles class. Now she had just gotten off the phone with Cathy, another in-group friend who revelled in gossip. They spent almost an hour speculating and rehashing every possible grievance they had against the pastor's wife.

Oddly enough, Joanne used to enjoy such conversations. She would get off the phone and feel a connectedness to her other friends. If it came at the expense of the pastor's wife and a few other self-righteous prudes, who cared? But now, more and more, Joanne found herself caring. This wasn't right and she knew it. But she was in so deep at this point, what could she do to make it different? Cut herself off from Vicki, Cathy, and the rest of the in-group?

A once unthinkable thought crossed her mind. What if she needed to go to the pastor's wife and others and ask them for forgiveness? Is that what God wanted her to do? How could God continue to love her after the childish way she behaved? Guilt compounded her fears, and she decided to go shopping to take herself out of the emotional whirlpool.

If you've been able to relate to our hypothetical friends so far, perhaps you can relate best of all to the feelings they experience after a fall. Whether we identify our sinfulness as addiction, giving in to temptation, acting impulsively, or calculated justification, we are still usually aware in our hearts of our sinfulness. Like a silent alarm tripped in our hearts, our awareness of our own sin produces a variety of conflicting emotions—guilt, anger, sadness, confusion, fear, regret, and numbness. *Which emotional current we choose to set sail on—the feelings we act on—often determines the extent we are willing to then know God, His forgiveness, and His mercy.* How we respond to demonstrative sin (actions, words, behavior patterns, etc.) as well as our inherent sinfulness, often determines whether we are moving toward God or away from Him, toward the Light or shrinking back into the darkness of our own selfish hearts.

This is, in fact, one of the keys to this entire life-process of repentance. It's a dividing line we have continually broached in the previous chapters. If our sinfulness is inherent, if the tension of living with our new redeemed nature and our old selfish nature is inescapable, if addictive tendencies are inevitable (but not unconquerable), truths which likely bear themselves out in your life already, then what do we do about them? What does it mean to turn toward God after giving in to sinful pleasures? Isn't that a little too convenient? Don't we risk abusing grace if we're always running back to God and asking forgiveness every time we sin?

What about this consuming swirl of emotions? Which ones are of the Holy Spirit, seeking to convict me of my sin and remind me of God's loving forgiveness? Which ones are of the Enemy, seeking to keep me down, wallowing in self-pity, self-recrimination, contempt, and isolation? Can we even tell the difference?

A BAROMETER OF FAITH

While numerous factors affect behavior, motivation, and change in people, the way people respond to their sin often exposes, more than anything else, their belief system and the extent to which they trust God. Think of your response before God when confronted with your sin as a kind of faith barometer. Do we dare believe that He can know the full measure of our wickedness and still love us?

Often our standards are exposed as higher than God's, an indication of our incredible arrogance, fear, and shame, not the noble righteousness which is His alone. This refusal to embrace God's forgiveness, to experience the perfect love that casts out fear, perpetuates the vicious cycle described in chapter 1. This cycle, while frustratingly self-defeating of our ultimate longings, keeps our wheels spinning in place, working so hard at self-awareness and measuring change that we shut out God. In our hearts we are so burdened by what we know we deserve for our sin, and so aware of how other humans might respond, that we refuse to believe God's goodness.

In fact, we often hate God's impossible standard of perfection because it forces us to seek His goodness and mercy and not our own abilities to save ourselves. Thus, when our sin is exposed, we believe He will say, "Aha! Now I've got you, and you're going to pay!" While His righteousness and absolute justice entitle Him to this accusation, we overlook the fact that His wrath has already been poured out in full intensity on His own Son. Unfathomable to our fallen imaginations, our Father chose to sacrifice a part of Himself, to abandon Christ at the cross, and excoriate our wickedness through the death of the only innocent man.

Embracing this fact frees us to love, to take our myopic lenses off ourselves and off our sin. When we chose to accept Christ as our holy bridge to the Father, we were restored as His children. Nevertheless, we have an ongoing need to appropriate this forgiveness, to experience the weight of grace permeating our lives down to our bones. While we'll examine more of the implications of embracing and extending forgiveness in the next chapter, we must realize this need of forgiveness as an ongoing turning point in our lives, a directional marker that points us back to our Father again and again.

1. What have you observed about the way people deal with their sin?
2. What do you usually feel after a fall? What do you do?

GOD'S COMPLAINT TO HOSEA

We must realize we are not the first nor the last to wrestle with knowing and loving our Creator. The entire history of Israel was one long wrestling match. The Israelites continually flirted with other idols, cut God off from their lives, and attempted to find life without Him. Yahweh continually, persistently reminded His people, despite their hardheartedness, of His goodness and willingness to receive them. One of the primary ways He communicated this to Israel was through prophets, individuals willing to be used as God's megaphones.

Hosea, one such prophet, spoke for God to chastise Israel and call her to repentance. Much of his unpopular job meant pointing out the sins of the people, their overt acts of treachery against their Creator. As the leading tribe of the nation, Ephraim incurred Jehovah's wrath on all the tribes who worshiped and offered sacrifices to Baal (Hosea 2:8-13). Ephraim's leaders also practiced poor foreign policy (5:8-15—"determined to follow man's command") and denied they were accumulating wealth dishonestly:

> Surely I have become rich,
> I have found wealth for myself;
> In all my labors they will find in me no iniquity,
> Which would be sin. (12:8)

Despite God's persistent pursuit and willingness to forgive, Israel continued to seek self-sufficiency. In fact, the most powerful picture of this rebellion and God's loving persistence is reflected in Hosea's narrative about his marriage to Gomer.

A known harlot (1:2), Gomer continued to stray even after she married and bore children. She sought out lovers who would provide her with both needs and luxuries (2:5-13). Nonetheless, after Hosea separated himself from her, God instructed His prophet to pursue her and buy her back, even though she had fallen about as low as one can go. There is both a tenderness and a firmness in the poignant words Hosea speaks to his wife: "You shall stay with me for many days. You shall not play the harlot, nor shall you have a man; so I will also be toward you" (3:3).

God extends the same message to the wayward nation.

Although Israel continued to rebuff Him, notice the important observation God makes concerning the way His people address their sinfulness:

> "Woe to them, for they have strayed from Me! ...
> I would redeem them, but they speak lies against Me.
> And they do not cry to Me from their heart
> When they wail on their beds;
> For the sake of grain and new wine they assemble
>   themselves,
> They turn away from Me.
> Although I trained and strengthened their arms,
> Yet they devise evil against Me.
> They turn, but not upward,
> They are like a deceitful bow;
> Their princes will fall by the sword
> Because of the insolence of their tongue.
> This will be their derision in the land of Egypt."
>   (7:13-16)

---

3. Think of a time when you've been rejected and hurt by a loved one. With this in mind, what do you suppose motivated God to continually pursue the rebellious Israel?
4. Can you relate to Israel's distance from God? Where do you turn when you don't turn "upward"?

LATERAL EMOTIONS

Notice the invitation God extends ("I would redeem them") and the options that present themselves, basically two. While viewing choices as either-or often oversimplifies complex issues, here it reflects God's truth: "They turn, but not upward." Bottom line, we can choose one of two directions when confronted with our sinfulness: lateral or vertical.

We can keep our sin on a lateral plane and scramble from emotion to emotion, technique to technique, and manage it ourselves. We can find idols or addictions and invest ourselves in them. We can ignore the problem and hope it goes away without consequences. We can justify our sin like a skillful attorney defending his client.

This lateral choice includes internal feelings and messages of guilt ("I know I've done a horrible thing; I must not tell anyone or get caught; I can't bear to face the consequences."), illegitimate shame ("I feel so bad, so guilty; I must be a horrible person; I must not let this be known."), denial ("I'm not so bad; there are others worse than me."), and self-contempt ("I am a horrible person; no one can handle how bad I really am; no one can forgive me, not even God."). Let's examine these emotions and their lateral effects one at a time.

Guilt and Shame
Often our first responses, guilt (the awareness of our sin) and shame (the feeling of humiliation from this awareness) trigger only self-pity and justification in our selfish, lateral zone. We feel sorry for ourselves because things aren't going our way. Our marriage is hard, the mortgage just went up, singleness feels unbearable, our bodies betray us with disease, and on and on our list goes. And who has been there for us? Haven't people always let us down, eventually? Hasn't God let us down by not giving us what we pray for? This "wailing upon our beds" keeps the focus on us and our problems. Our comfort and pleasure matter most in this perspective.

Now, God does not ask us to pretend things are better than they are. Scripture consistently instructs us to cry out to Him, to share our heart's fears, worries, and sorrows, along with joys and praises. In the Hosea passage He declares, "They do not cry to Me from their heart." Our Father wants all of us and accepts us in our humanity, although not because of it. In other words, God accepts us as men and women but is committed to changing us into "little Christs" as C. S. Lewis put it. We must die to self and come alive in Christ.

If your life is like mine, however, I frequently find it easier to wail on my bed than cry out to God with an honesty that requires me to suffer in the present sinful world and still yearn for His glory in Heaven.

In order to wail on our beds, we take the first step of experiencing guilt (usually unavoidable if we are redeemed image-bearers alive to God's Spirit) by realizing that we have failed, have violated God's standard of goodness, have hurt others and actively made ourselves the center of the universe. Guilt is a powerful catalyst; it usually forces us closer to choosing what we will do with ourselves and what we believe about God.

If our guilt only propels us into feeling bad, then we're still in lateral movement. Our shame then amounts to remorse for being exposed to ourselves and others; however, underneath smolders a deep-seated anger, even hatred, at God for requiring such impossible perfection. Oswald Chambers explains, "Remorse is never repentance, remorse is the rebellion of man's own pride which will not agree with God's judgment on sin but accuses God because He has made His laws too stern and holy."[1]

Denial

This remorse often spurs us to downplay our sin by either justifying it or ignoring it. Both amount to denial, which is really nothing more than the ultimate self-deception that we can slip a lie past God.

One vivid example of such denial occurs in Acts. Ananias and Sapphira sell their property to share with the young body of believers, but hold back some of the money for themselves. Peter confronts Ananias with a barrage of questions concerning his deceit: "How did Satan get you to lie to the Holy Spirit and secretly keep back part of the price of the field? What got into you to pull a trick like this? You didn't lie to men but to God." Without responding, Ananias falls over dead and is promptly carried out. When Sapphira enters, unaware of what's happened, she maintains the collusion, and after similar questions from Peter, she too slumps forward. "By this time the whole church and, in fact, everyone who heard of these things had a healthy respect for God. They knew God was not to be trifled with" (Acts 5:11, MESSAGE).

Denying our sin is lying to God. Even if we are not as brazen as this deceitful couple, we still must realize that we never fool God. If we choose denial, we cut ourselves off from His goodness and His presence because He is Truth and will not tolerate our lies. Indeed, He will not be trifled with, and a healthy respect, an awe, of His righteousness and goodness should be part of our worshipful awareness of Him. However, our approach should not be an obsessive legalism and rule-keeping based on the terror of a hostage, but rather the grateful, loving loyalty of a prisoner set free.

Contempt and Ambivalence
Since denial can be difficult to maintain—maintaining illusions is exhausting—we often graduate into more pervasive strategies for managing our sin. Thus, another self-defeating method involves the combination of shame—feeling remorseful, primarily because we were caught and/or have to suffer unpleasant consequences—and hatred at God for requiring such obedience from us. Such a combination often leads to contempt, an angry hatred at self and others for the exposure or lack of exposure of your sin.

In the midst of this contemptuous anger, we still long to change, we just don't want it to be so painful or require suffering. When our contempt mixes with our desire to change, to know God regardless of the cost, we often feel ambivalent. This ambivalence again reflects our desires to seek God and avoid God, to know His loving mercy and to fear His wrath. Like a child who has wandered off from his father at a busy intersection, we fear his justifiable anger for our rebellion but long for our daddy's arms in the midst of an overwhelming crowd of strangers. Rarely do we allow such a tension to remind us of our Father's longing for relationship and restoration, His gift of grace. As we have seen, that requires humility, dependence, and faith. Typically, as Chambers points out in the aforementioned quote, it often comes more natural to shake our fist in God's face for requiring a perfect standard in a fallen world. This allows us to remain justified in our sinful flight.

Rarely, however, are we this direct with our angry self-justifications. We subvert our rage or ambivalence and try to pretend it isn't there. Nonetheless, it still emerges in off-the-cuff barbs as well as direct assaults. Such contempt often works well for Christians because it allows us to acknowledge our sin, perhaps even to ask for forgiveness, without having to own responsibility. We play a game of change but internally hate the rules, so we continue to justify playing by our own rules.

When confronted with lovingly harsh words that call us to a higher standard, whether from a spouse, our children, or a trusted friend, we nod in agreement but inwardly seethe. "Yes, I suppose I could have a problem with anger (or whatever). Can you give me some examples of what you're talking about?" Thus, our contempt emerges as we force the other to prove his or her case. Depending on how strong her examples and her ability to articulate them, we often get ourselves off the hook, maintaining self-justification. Or, if backed into a corner, we might quickly feign remorse and declare, "I'm sorry. Forgive me?" when we're actually thinking, "I hate you for seeing my sin just as I hate God for requiring such obedience. Who do you think you are to expose my sin, anyway?"

We can also turn our contempt inward. This usually results in more anger, terror, hopelessness, and despair. If we can't save ourselves, if others can't be counted on, if we can't turn to God because He's too holy and righteous, then what can we do? Consequently, we return to idols and perpetuate the futile cycle; we refuse to trust in God's goodness toward us, and we refuse to hope beyond what we can see or understand ourselves (which is not hope at all, but merely speculation and projection). We become depressed and despairing, isolating ourselves further and further from others and God.

Recall the example of Joanne, who struggles with gossiping

in order to maintain "friendships" with the other gossipers and thus avoid the intense loneliness that gnaws at her soul. Her thinking might go something like this in such a despairing cycle: "Well, I must not be very likable if I can't create the kind of rich relationships I long for. Something must be wrong with me. Friendships just don't last—something always happens. They move away, I move away, they get married, we drift apart, we lose common interests. And other people? They sure don't pursue me for very long. I even hate that I need them.

"But I hate being alone even more. If God loves and cares about me, why am I so lonely? Why doesn't He do something about it? I've sure learned that I can't sit around and wait on Him to bring friends into my life.

"I guess that takes me back to doing whatever it takes to make people like me. I'll gossip, follow their leads, try to be whatever or whoever it takes for them to let me feel like I belong. It's the best I can do. It's the best that's available in the situation."

Judas
A biblical portrait of this deadly spiral emerges from the betrayer Judas. Perhaps there is no better picture of self-absorbed remorse than Judas' suicide. After having plotted to hand over Jesus to the Pharisees for thirty pieces of silver, the forlorn disciple realizes the weight of his betrayal:

> Judas, the one who betrayed him, realized that Jesus was doomed. Overcome with remorse, he gave back the thirty silver coins to the high priests, saying, "I've sinned. I've betrayed an innocent man."
>
> They said, "What do we care? That's *your* problem!"
>
> Judas threw the silver coins into the Temple and left. Then he went out and hung himself. (Matthew 27:3-6, MESSAGE)

If we find it hard to imagine being in Judas' shoes and taking any other action than the noose he chose, then we have not faced the full force of our own betrayals of Christ. Even Judas was not beyond redemption, but it required facing the pain of a shattered heart, the humility of his sin before God, and the desire to know God more than to alleviate his guilt. Peter's denial was just as much a betrayal as Judas', but Peter embraced the forgiveness offered at the heart of the gospel. Judas, however, pridefully maintained a higher standard than God's; he chose suicide out of hopelessness, the ultimate selfish act.

5. How often do you wrestle with guilt and shame? Where do they usually lead you?
6. How would you describe the difference between "wailing on your bed" and "crying out to God"? How have you experienced this difference?
7. When have you experienced contempt?

CHOOSING THE VERTICAL

The other choice, the vertical journey, of which accepting Christ is the major turning point, involves acknowledging our sinfulness and our neediness before God. It's coming to our senses, like the prodigal, and realizing the truth about who we are, what we have access to, and most importantly, who God is. He is not the benign grandfather of our imaginations, not the tyrannical drill sergeant, not the detached cosmic observer, not the absent father of our childhoods. He is the God of the Universe, the Trinity of Abba, Son, and Spirit. He is unfathomable and mysterious. He is neither powerless or legalistic. He is alive. He runs down the path to meet us in the tenderest embrace, no matter how many times we stutter-step, stumble, or spit in His face.

Knowing this kind of intimacy with God requires feeling many of the same emotions, perhaps even more so than choosing to handle it yourself. Too often, we believe that it means feeling fewer negative emotions, but this is merely wishful thinking. These same powerful emotions—guilt, fear, shame, and despair—which we shun as dangerous, sinful or potentially sinful, and uncontrollable, are, in fact, glaring road signs pointing back to our need for God.

> Our culture presumes that emotions are amoral—neither right nor wrong. According to this perspective, it's not what we feel that's potentially sinful, but rather what we do with our feelings. The problem with this view is its assumption that some element of our personality escaped the consequences of the Fall.
>
> It seems more accurate to say that our feelings are not any more or less sinful than our thoughts, desires, and behaviors. But God can use our emotions to disclose sin through revealing the depths of our battle with Him.[2]

Therefore, our emotions, especially the ones we quickly tag as unpleasant, even ugly, have the greatest potential to call us to repentance. As we have seen, though, embracing this process means setting our pride and selfishness aside, and suffering the pain and brokenness that come when we feel both the crushing weight of our sin and the ineffable joy and gratitude of experiencing God's grace.

When we desire to know God rather than simply use Him to feel better about ourselves and our problems, then we make vertical choices. We still experience guilt and shame over our transgressions, but we choose to embrace those feelings, allowing the Holy Spirit to remind us of our loving Father, of His goodness and mercy. This direction takes us away from the self-consciousness of lateral feelings of contempt, denial, martyristic shame and fearful guilt and into the brokenheartedness of repentance.

In pursuing vertical choices, our guilt then becomes conviction, an awareness of our wrongdoing and its consequences. We feel the full weight of our wrongdoing and the damage it does to others, but most of all to our Abba. We are reminded of our continual need for Him, and rather than despising this fact, we admit the full longing of our redeemed hearts to know Him, to feel His embrace, to serve Him.

This same heart conviction transforms shame into sorrow. We grieve the ways we hurt others and the selfishness that permeates our being. We allow ourselves to acknowledge our sin before others without downplaying its gravity. We face up to consequences and make restitution as a gesture of the grace we've experienced from our Father.

As we embrace such brokenness and allow the Spirit to activate our repentant heart, we become more willing to suffer. Rather than arming ourselves with denial or contempt, remorse or regret, we suffer the tension of our fallenness and our redemption.

> For we know that the whole creation groans and suffers the pains of childbirth together until now. And not only this, but also we ourselves, having the first fruits of the Spirit, even we ourselves groan within ourselves, waiting eagerly for our adoption as sons, the redemption of our body. (Romans 8:22-23)

We seek with all our being to love and glorify our Father, to hope for Heaven, to embrace the full wonder of Christ. We manifest this fervent desire with a loving passion and grace for others. We share ourselves with them, take risks to know them and be known by them, and always point back to our Father's glory, wonder, and mystery.

This is not easy; on the contrary, it's next to impossible, but neither is it lofty rhetoric. Indeed, we have the Holy Spirit to aid us even when it feels impossible to us.

> Meanwhile, the moment we get tired in the waiting, God's Spirit is right alongside helping us along. If we don't know how or what to pray, it doesn't matter. He does our praying in and for us, making prayer out of our wordless sighs, our aching groans. He knows us far better than we know ourselves. (Romans 8:26-27, MESSAGE)

Unfortunately, we often feel that repentance, embracing forgiveness, and relying on the Spirit are impossible. They sound like wonderful concepts, but they become difficult to imagine concretely in the midst of experiences and emotions. They don't happen when we want them to, we don't feel them as we think they should feel, and we continue to struggle.

However, the sorrow and conviction that facilitate repentance involve smaller, daily choices. We must cultivate habits of solitude (alone time with God), prayer (talking with Him), Bible study (learning about Him and His stories), and other spiritual disciplines. We must carve out time in our lives to be alone with ourselves and our Lord. We must make time in order to allow ourselves to sorrow over sin, to reflect on our neediness of grace, to soak in the Father's mercy. While we must not ignore our feelings and use spiritual disciplines as formulaic busywork, we can only transcend our feelings when we return to our anchor commitment to Christ and allow our Father to forgive and embrace us. This requires time. (We'll explore these habits further in chapter 8.)

A REPENTANT HEART

Vivid portraits of this repentant response punctuate Scripture. In fact, one of the sharpest pictures occurs side-by-side with that of Judas. Peter, ever zealous and committed, found himself doing what he longed never to do: deny his Savior. In Gethsemane, Christ tells His followers they will be scattered after His death.

> Peter broke in, "Even if everyone else falls to pieces on account of you, I won't."
>
> "Don't be so sure," Jesus said. "This very night, before the rooster crows up the dawn, you will deny me three times."
>
> Peter protested, "Even if I had to die with you, I would never deny you." All the others said the same thing. (Matthew 26:33-35, MESSAGE)

Jesus then prays out of the depths of His sorrow and asks the disciples to keep a prayer vigil with Him.

> When he came back to his disciples, he found them sound asleep. He said to Peter, "Can't you stick it out with me a single hour? Stay alert; be in prayer so you don't wander into temptation without even knowing you're in danger. There is a part of you that is eager, ready for anything in God. But there's another part that's as lazy as an old dog sleeping by the fire." (Matthew 26:40-41, MESSAGE)

Christ points out the duality of our condition once again. Like Romans 6–8, which we examined in chapter 1, Jesus' observation reminds us of the tension between our fallen nature of selfish inclination and our redeemed heart fixed on God. So often our fickleness is astounding; we can be praying one moment and swearing at our mate the next. Christ's instruction to stay alert and be in prayer, while not formulaic, reminds us of our relationship with the Father. We should know ourselves well enough to know we will fail, and we should know God well enough to accept His loving mercy. And as we continue with the story, we see Peter doing just that.

> All this time [while Jesus was being charged and mocked before Caiaphas], Peter was sitting out in the courtyard. One servant girl came up to him and said, "You were with Jesus the Galilean."
>
> In front of everybody there, he denied it. "I don't know what you're talking about."
>
> As he moved over toward the gate, someone else said to the people there, "This man was with Jesus the Nazarene."
>
> Again he denied it, salting his denial with an oath: "I swear, I never laid eyes on the man."
>
> Shortly after that, some bystanders approached Peter.

"You've got to be one of them. Your accent gives you away."

Then he got really nervous and swore. "I don't know the man!"

Just then a rooster crowed. Peter remembered what Jesus had said: "Before the rooster crows, you will deny me three times." He went out and cried and cried and cried. (Matthew 26:69-75, MESSAGE)

When was the last time you cried and cried and cried over your sin? If you're like me, most of the time I work hard to avoid this level of grief and neediness. However, these are two key ingredients in transforming shame and guilt into repentance. Otherwise, we end up paralyzed in a selfish stupor of ambivalence or else we are driven to soul suicide like Judas.

While we are not informed of Peter's thoughts and feelings, it seems evident that he is immediately broken by recalling Jesus' words and facing his sin. He spends little or no time justifying his actions as we might: "But I had to protect myself. What good am I in spreading the gospel if I'm dead? I had to be convincing. That's it, I was acting a part. I would never really deny You, Lord. You know that, right?"

Instead, Peter not only recognizes his sin, but takes responsibility for it. He is crushed by his failure. He passionately loves his friend, mentor, and Messiah, and he has denied even knowing Him. His tears are not for himself, but for the disappointing hurt that Jesus must have felt, a pain He was surely aware of before it even happened. This disciple does not wail on his bed for God to forgive him so he can feel better. Peter cries out of the depths of his soul over having hurt the One he loves most.

Although I have chosen to present them in reverse order, it's important to mention that the Scripture passage that immediately follows Peter's denial and grief depicts Judas' diametric response to a similar betrayal. This juxtaposes the two men's responses in the sharpest terms; we go from seeing Peter's awareness of sin and his subsequent anguish to seeing Judas' epiphany and his decision to end his life.

Nineteenth-century writer William Nevins compares the two this way:

> There are two kinds of repentance: one is that of Judas, the other that of Peter; the one is ice broken, the other ice melted. Repentance unto life will be repentance in the life.[3]

This ice metaphor seems particularly apt, for if we turn to ourselves and our standards in order to repent, then we will indeed be broken and fragmented. The ultimate arrogance is to think that we are so bad or have sinned so heinously that God cannot or will not forgive us. As James reminds us, "There is only one Lawgiver and Judge, the One who is able to save and to destroy; but who are you who judge your neighbor?" (4:12). This applies equally to ourselves: who are we to arrogantly judge ourselves and decide that we are worse (or better) than anyone else? We must live out of faith, out of trusting in God's Grace, or else we will continually divide ourselves and choose self over God.

How did Peter live after such a haunting betrayal of his Master? Grace-fully. After His resurrection, Jesus spoke with His disciples several times. John's Gospel relates the meeting at the beach of the Sea of Galilee. The apostles are fishing unsuccessfully when a stranger on the beach instructs them to cast on the right side for a huge haul. They realize then that it's their Master. Peter exuberantly dives into the water and swims ashore, even though their boat was only about a hundred yards away. There is no hint of reluctance to face the Lord he had betrayed, no sheepishness, no shame, no fear. He knows the character, the being, of the Lord he serves.

After this beachside breakfast, Jesus questioned Peter three times: "Do you love me?" Peter replies, "Lord, you know I do." Jesus then responds, "Then tend my sheep." And as verified by other New Testament letters, including his own, Peter does indeed live a life of shepherding the infant church. Eugene Peterson describes Peter as a "breath of fresh air" for his bold, confident, and humble leadership. "By virtue of his position, he was easily the most powerful figure in the Christian community. And his energetic preaching, ardent prayer, bold healing, and wise direction confirmed the trust placed in him."[4]

Peter lived out of the grace he experienced. And while his thrice denial was likely a powerful benchmark of his faith, he continued living out his repentance, his faith, rather than viewing God's mercy as a one-shot acquittal. Thus, his advice to Christians in his own letters seems especially pertinent and authoritative:

> Because Jesus was raised from the dead, we've been
> given a brand-new life and have everything to live for,
> including a future in heaven—and the future starts now!
> Don't lazily slip back into those old grooves of evil,
> doing just what you feel like doing. You've had a taste of
> God. Now, like infants at the breast, drink deep of God's
> pure kindness. Then you'll grow up mature and whole in
> God. (1 Peter 1:3-4,14; 2:1-3; MESSAGE)

Peter's life provides a remarkable picture of what it means to live out of a repentant heart, to taste grace through God's kindness and go forward, toward Him, toward Heaven. This kind of living is not euphoric by any means; in fact, it requires more suffering than living selfishly in denial or escapism. But the intimacy, joy, and peace it produces have substance to them, yielded from the maturity of continually exercising faith.

Life will not be easier living with a repentant heart, but it will be more deeply satisfying and rewarding as we glorify our Creator by living out who He has redeemed us to be.

JOURNALING THE JOURNEY

From My Journal

I hate that I feel things so deeply. It's much more of a curse than a blessing; most men seem more in control, even if that means appearing insensitive. Although I know these men have feelings too, I always feel like my emotions work against me and my relationship with God. For example, I say something harsh to Dotti and immediately feel guilty. But then rather than feeling sad over how this must hurt her, I withdraw and find some busy task to take me out of this uncomfortable feeling. I hate that! By trying to stay in control and emulating these men I have in mind, I'm not only rejecting a powerful, godly gift—my feelings—but I'm also using them to justify sinning.

I do have hope, though. As much as I often hate how I feel, I am thankful that it leads me back to God, back to needing His forgiveness, as well as needing my wife's forgiveness. It humbles me. And while this may not feel comfortable and "in control," it does remind me of my desire to live out of my redeemed heart, emotions and all.

For Your Journal

Think through what you've been feeling as you read this book, even this chapter. What does it stir in you—hope, fear, confusion, anger, ambivalence, joy, guilt, sorrow?

Brainstorm a list of the emotions you've felt concerning your relationship with God over the past few weeks. Now go back over your list and write a paragraph about each one. Where do your emotions take you? Where do you want them to take you?

5

PENANCE VERSUS REPENTANCE

—

Michelle smiled and raised her hand to volunteer for the upcoming Missions Banquet. It would be a challenge to say the least, on top of her already overbooked schedule. She knew her husband wouldn't like it, but she felt compelled to do everything possible to facilitate God's work. Brian had recently challenged her on this, and she'd spouted back that he just didn't understand. His response still echoed in her mind, "Your church work defines you. Somehow you think volunteering for every committee will make up for the fact that you're never here for me and the kids!"

David's mind wandered to his family as the pilot announced the flight had been cleared for landing. This week, like the other twenty or so this year, had flown by quickly, with appointment after meeting after seminar. *I hate being away,* he thought, *missing the boys' soccer games and time alone with Sally. But somebody has to pay the bills.* David thought of all the extra hours he put in, how in some ways work was easier to manage than home. *I'll make it up to them,* he continued thinking.

But a nagging thought lanced his moment of relief: what if there was really no way to compensate for an absent dad and husband? What if his workaholism—including all the Nintendos, beach vacations, and new minivans it afforded—could never compensate for his lack of love, leadership, and presence? Hadn't he turned over a new leaf at the first of the year and vowed to reduce his time away? Hadn't he recommitted himself to being a more godly husband and dad? But had anything really changed? As the tires hit the runway, David wondered what actions he would have to take if he really wanted to change.

All of us find ways to try to make our lives work without having to depend on God. As we saw in the previous chapter, how we respond to the emotions of repentance—feelings like guilt, shame, remorse, and regret—often reveals as well as determines how we perceive God and our relationship with Him. Unfortunately, in our selfishness we often wallow in these emotions, fixated on our pain, discomfort, and the consequences of our sin. This, however, is not repentance, nor the emotions of repentance: guilt turned to conviction, shame to sorrow, regret to suffering.

The actions we take based on these feelings and our perceptions of how change works also tend to go one of two directions: toward self or toward God, horizontal or vertical. When we remain fixed on ourselves, eager to distance ourselves from the reality and emotions of our sin, we tend to act horizontally in stages of denial, self-sufficiency, and penance. Since we are more concerned with removing the problem, often certain specific sins or addictions, than with knowing God, we can only view Him out of our anger and frustration at His seeming indifference, incapability, or unwillingness to aid us in our struggle. Thus, we keep our eyes fixed on ourselves and our resources engaged in overcoming sin as we see fit.

THE DOUBLE-MINDEDNESS OF DENIAL

If we say that we have no sin, we are deceiving ourselves, and the truth is not in us. (1 John 1:8)

One of the quickest responses we use to escape the reality and
consequences of our sin is denial. Denial is pretending something
isn't true, such as, "Calories don't count if you eat them in the
car." Denial easily becomes dissociation—separating ourselves
psychologically from present surroundings and events. Dissociation may be as simple as living in daydreams to escape real life
or as drastic as blacking out during traumatic experiences.

Because the weight of our transgressions often feels unbear-
ably crushing and shameful, we try to separate ourselves as
quickly as possible from the physical, as well as emotional,
"scene of the crime." We separate our "sinful self"—what often
feels like a combination of our fleshly yearnings and internal
emotions—from our "redeemed self."

This acute self-division resembles what James calls being
"double-minded" (James 1:7-8), asking God yet still doubting
Him. We become torn between the desires we feel and our disappointment that God has not removed our struggles on one
hand, and the shimmer of hope that He is indeed good and faithful and committed to loving us beyond our wildest dreams on
the other. This tension often drives us back to the sinful rebellion
of self-management.

Let me provide an example of this kind of acute denial and
division of self. I once counseled a married man who habitually,
secretly, frequented singles bars and adult bookstores, coming
as close to physical encounters with other women as possible
without actual touch. As we discussed Rob's anguish over his
secret sin, he confessed that he often felt like two different people,
or like one man juggling two worlds of his own creation—his
Christian, married family-man world and his secret world of fantasy and flirtation.

I asked Rob if they ever overlapped and he replied, "I work

hard to make sure they never do. Sometimes I'll be driving away from a topless bar, knowing I'll be home in fifteen minutes acting like nothing's going on. Then when I walk in my front door, I'll smile and play with the kids and kiss my wife, never revealing the shame and fear swirling inside. I hate it, but it's what I do." I then asked Rob how he responded when the two worlds overlapped; for instance, if he happened to think of his wife and children in the middle of his fantasy. "No," he answered, "I make sure that I cut off the players from each world. I couldn't bear to think of the effect my struggle would have on my wife and kids—even my friends—if it ever came out. I cut them all off; I can't think about them or about consequences of the two worlds colliding."

One of my goals with Rob became to force him to realize that he is indeed only one man living in one world and that dividing himself between two worlds was really nothing more than a complex system of sinful denial. His fervent efforts at dissociating from both sets of conflicting feelings—his love and commitment to God, his wife, and family versus his addictive sexual attractions—were destroying his soul. I made it clear that if he continued to live in self-deception, a system that wasn't working too well, he would never know the depths of God's grace or the fullness of the man he was created to be. He would live a divided, double-minded life, paralyzed between living selfishly or suffering biblically.

He chose the latter, and in such a situation, his desire to break out of denial, to shatter the lies, became the first step in rebuilding his life and rediscovering the incredible grace of God.

Perhaps you view Rob as an extreme example. But how many of us find ourselves acting, even feeling, more "spiritual" on Sundays than during the rest of the week? I believe many of us often feel divided between who we pretend to be (a "perfect" Christian who has his or her life together) and who we really are (a struggling pilgrim who continually needs God).

In fact, many teachers and preachers often encourage us to "remember our true identity in Christ" as a strategy to overcome sin and struggles. While this is true and important, remembering our true identity in Christ will not take away our struggle in this life. We are redeemed, changed, reborn in the birth of the Spirit, but we are still in process by virtue of being human and on this side of Paradise. Any other attempt at living, either in a severe addiction like Rob's or in the dualism of dividing ourselves between our smooth Christian front and our real struggles, amounts to denying the ultimate truth of our Father. This denial, while attempting to shield us from what feels like unbearable pain and shame, becomes self-defeating, keeping us from our deepest desires. When we live in denial, we basically refuse God the opportunity to love us as He longs to do.

1. Look up James 1:5-8. How is the double-minded person described? How does this person's instability hinder the repentance process? How does asking God for wisdom aid in repentance?
2. What are ways you attempt to hide your real struggles from yourself and others? How much pressure do you feel presently to be a Christian "who has it all together"?

PENANCE: AN ATTEMPT TO COMPENSATE

> Where then is boasting? It is excluded. By what kind of law? Of works? No, but by a law of faith. For we maintain that a man is justified by faith apart from works of the Law. (Romans 3:27-28)

Another way we attempt to refuse the gift of grace is through compensation, or penance. While we all likely have pockets of denial in our lives, we are still haunted by the knowledge of our sin, and no amount of denial can or will distance us far enough from it. Bottom line, we know we're not perfect and can't pretend to be. So when denial doesn't work, rather than cover up our sin as if it isn't there, we try to compensate for it.

This notion is as old as the church itself. In fact, one of the major criticisms Martin Luther leveled against the Catholic Church was its system of confession, penance, and absolution for the forgiveness of sins rather than simply accepting the grace-gift of Christ's sacrifice on the cross. This penance system was not only theologically erroneous according to Luther and other Protestant Reformers, but it had long since been corrupted by greed and power within the Church. People could literally buy their forgiveness in Luther's time, if they were well-connected or wealthy enough.

This notion of penance takes a foundational truth—that people should act differently if they have indeed experienced a heart-change by God's grace and their acceptance of Him—and makes it a requirement that can be processed and managed. Much of the problem Luther pointed to involved having someone else—the priest, bishop, or other church leader—decide what one's penance should be. One kept track of his or her various sins, confessed them regularly to a higher church intermediary, and was given specific tasks (often including financial contributions to the Church) in order to complete the process of forgiveness. For instance, two lies, three prideful thoughts, and one theft might equate to saying four "Hail Marys," two "Our Fathers," and increasing your tithe.

While this grocery-list mind-set seems as unbiblical now as it did then, we still often believe we can make up for our misdeeds. My first response to such a notion is: If only it were that simple! We could tell someone else, someone who repre-sents God directly, who could then give us a formula for expe-riencing forgiveness and living the repentant life. But this amounts to distancing, objectifying, and manipulating the most intense and personal of relationships, our bond to our Abba Father. While confession to others can and does play an essen-tial part of the repentance process (see chapter 7 on commu-nity and accountability), we have sinned against God most of all and yet, through Christ, have direct access to our Father. We must remember that Christ bears the wrath of His Father's Law and this atonement (Jesus paying for what we rightly deserve) allows us to approach our Father out of His love for us. We still approach with fear and trembling, fully aware of what we deserve, and yet confident of our Father's goodness, patience, and His joy at our restoration. All of this is to say that no human has God's authority to grant forgiveness, and there is no method other than Christ to appropriate grace for the mess of our transgressions.

My second thought about a system of penance and management is this: While we often long for the kind of merit system that penance falsely attempts to provide, thank God it does not exist! We would fail miserably ever to compensate for the damage of our sins—it's impossible. A merit system would condemn us to excruciating punishment for eternity.

And thirdly, if indeed we could make up for our sins so that our good actions counterbalanced our bad, then we could basically control our lives. If we wanted to rob the Chase Manhattan, we could, so long as we then spent the next ten years serving food in a homeless shelter (or whatever we deemed appropriate compensation). We could justify about anything we did. Far worse, however, is that we would not need God. We would cut Him out of our lives since we could manage so well without Him that we wouldn't even need His forgiveness. We could simply do whatever it took to have the credit column outweigh the debit side.

This attempt to avoid needing God whitewashes our sins. We're either incredibly arrogant or naive to believe our account of good deeds could ever catch up to a list of our selfish, sinful acts and thoughts.

"There is none righteous, not even one;
There is none who understands,
There is none who seeks for God;
All have turned aside, together they have become useless;

There is none who does good,
There is not even one." (Romans 3:10-12)

Penance also overlooks our inherent neediness, the sinful nature we have had from conception (Psalm 51:5).

The truth is, we cannot not need God. We must be dependent on Him continuously every moment of our lives. Faced with the uncertainty of life, the harshness of unforseen circumstances, the pain of even the best relationships, we often acknowledge this conceptually but balk in our hearts.

Jenny, a mother and homemaker in her thirties, describes her awareness of this tendency this way: "I feel like I have two dates for the same night. One date is with God, and I'm supposed to meet Him at this quiet place of worship in the deepest part of me. But He might not show up, not in the way I want Him to. And if He does show up, He lovingly reminds me that He and I are married; this isn't a casual first date. He wants and has all of me. I'm terrified of what He requires.

"The alternative to this date is one of my own making. I call the shots and control my 'date' that I know will make me feel better, whether it's overeating, going on a shopping binge, gossiping, or withholding myself from what my husband requires. While this feels more like an inconsequential, one-night-stand kind of date, it can't possibly satisfy me the way my relationship with my Father does. But at least this kind of date feels controllable; I don't face the fear of the unknown like I do on my date with God."

This candid response reveals the struggle most of us feel between penance and repentance. We want to change, and we know something is required of us, but then instead of waiting on God, expecting His divine, surprising, unpredictable intervention and presence, we try to make it all happen without Him. We would do it all if He'd simply give us His stamp of approval. But as we've experienced personally, read in Scripture, and seen in this chapter, the repentance process, and acting out of it authentically, doesn't work this way.

3. Why is it so tempting to try to compensate for our sin? Why is this impossible?
4. Can you relate to Jenny's two "dates"? In what ways do you attempt to make life work apart from God?

CONFESSION: A BROKEN AND CONTRITE HEART

If we confess our sins, he is faithful and just and will forgive us our sins and purify us from all unrighteousness. (1 John 1:9, NIV)

So how do we act out of a repentant heart? If we know we can never compensate for our sin, no matter how hard we try, and if we know that we shouldn't keep on sinning cavalierly and wait passively for God's grace, what do we do?

As we've seen, the starting point is an awareness of our sin and need that drives us to bended knees and a humbled heart before God. We face temptation, we struggle honestly with addictions or idolatrous longings and behavior, and view those as reminders of needing God's presence, of our redemption through Christ, of our longing for Heaven. We must face the depravity within ourselves or we will never fully realize the unfathomable import of the grace we are given. As starving men and women, we appreciate the bounty of God's glorious feast only as we feel the pangs of hunger rumble in our empty bellies and smell the tantalizing aroma of His love. How, then, do we take the first bite?

David's Sin

The Old Testament shows us, in the adulterous struggles of David, a dynamic portrait of what our sinfulness should cost us and of God's incredible mercy that cancels the debt for us. With his personal charisma, along with his authority as king of Israel, David had numerous wives and concubines, and could have had virtually any woman he wanted. However, his wandering eyes and passionate heart settled on the bathing Bathsheba. The fact that she was married to Uriah, who was off fighting a war that David started, made no difference. When Bathsheba became pregnant as a result of their union, David compounded his sin by covering it up. In fact, his denial extended to the point of murder. David sent a letter to his military commander Joab, instructing: "Place Uriah in the front line of the fiercest battle and withdraw from him, so that he may be struck down and die" (2 Samuel 11:15).

When Bathsheba's time for mourning her husband's death ended, David took her as his wife. So far, so good—David's plan was working. However, "the thing that David had done was evil in the sight of the LORD" (2 Samuel 11:27). There's no fooling our Father, and David, despite being a powerful and courageous king, was not exempt from God's Law. God then sent the prophet Nathan to confront David and expose his wickedness and deceit. Nathan wisely chooses indirection (remember, David's already killed once to keep his secret) in his rebuke. He tells David the hypothetical story of two men, one rich with many flocks and herds, and one poor with only one little ewe lamb. When a traveler stops for a meal, the rich man is unwilling to pick from his own flock and instead slaughters the poor man's only lamb.

David was furious at the injustice of the situation and replied to Nathan: "As the LORD lives, surely the man who has done this deserves to die. And he must make restitution for the lamb fourfold, because he did this thing and had no compassion" (2 Samuel 12:5-6). Nathan then lowers the boom; he points the finger at David for his adultery, murder, and deceit and informs him of the consequences according to the Lord. David can no longer cover up his sinfulness and has in fact hung himself. His anger and zeal at punishing the offender in Nathan's story reveal a glimmer of what he knows he rightfully deserves himself.

Facing the Truth

While the consequences of David's sin are severe, including the death of the child he and Bathsheba produced, we must not overlook the fact that David did indeed repent and continue to serve his Lord. David's prayer of humble sorrow and repentance is preserved for us in Psalm 51. Often used as a model of prayerful repentance for many centuries, this timeless poem continues to guide and inspire us today with insight into what repentance really means. David begins by asking for God's grace and lovingkindness:

> Be gracious to me, O God, according to Thy
>   lovingkindness;
> According to the greatness of Thy compassion blot out
>   my transgressions.
> Wash me thoroughly from my iniquity,
> And cleanse me from my sin. (verses 1-2)

His heart's attitude is one of humility and a desperate longing for restoration and cleansing. This approach neither minimizes his sin by seeking God's forgiveness as a token, nor does it maximize the sin as unforgivable by making his standard greater than God's. David feels both the weight of what he's done and who he is before his righteous God, as well as the hope of mercy, restoration, and renewal before his loving Father.

David continues:

> For I know my transgressions,
> And my sin is ever before me.
> Against Thee, Thee only, I have sinned,
> And done what is evil in Thy sight,
> So that Thou art justified when Thou dost speak,
> And blameless when Thou dost judge. (verses 3-4)

This admission of wrongdoing is in sharp contrast to the complex system of denial David used to cover up his sin. We must remember that this is the same man who instructed that another man die to keep his sin concealed. David realizes that his sin, along with all our sin, is ultimately an affront against the Creator. While others will be sinned against, affected by, and damaged by our selfishness, ultimately we come back to our relationship with the Father. Like the prodigal, do we demand our inheritance now and insist on controlling and spending it ourselves? Or do we dare partake in a deeper joy and hope than any immediate gratification on earth can provide? Do we rebel or obey the Father who loves us to the extreme of sacrificing His Son?

Our sin, while often retaliating against others, boils down to shaking our clenched fist in God's face. Think back to our definition of remorse from the last chapter, and the way we hate God for requiring such perfection and obedience from us. This leads to bitterness and contempt for self, others, and especially God. But notice that David is not hating God for His holy standard, but acknowledging His righteousness and the absolute appropriateness of that standard. Our Father remains more than justified and blameless in His goodness and perfection. He is God. We are human beings, men and women born in His image. We sin, no matter how we deny, cover up, compensate, ignore, or describe it. He does not, no matter how we perceive, misperceive, or fail to understand His will and design for us and the world.

Seeking Wisdom

David continues by acknowledging another point of tension between himself and God:

> Behold, I was brought forth in iniquity,
> And in sin my mother conceived me.
> Behold, Thou dost desire truth in the innermost being,
> And in the hidden part Thou wilt make me know wisdom.
> (verses 5-6)

Because of the rebellious choice of Adam and Eve, we all suffer the consequences—inheriting the human condition of sinfulness and living outside the garden. Nonetheless, this was not God's hope or intention in giving Adam and Eve (and us) free will; He still desires us to know Him and His truth all the way down to our souls, to the core of our being. Basically, David describes, in another way, the tension between who we are presently and who God is redeeming us into, the tension of sanctification. David's acknowledgment of this tension reminds us once again that we both need God inherently (from conception), and that God is committed to redeeming us (long before conception).

Also, note that God desires us to "know wisdom" in our innermost beings (verse 6), a reminder of what James instructs: "If any of you lacks wisdom, let him ask of God . . . in faith without any doubting" (1:5-6). This points to the importance of hope and its actualization, faith, versus the self-divided instability of "double-mindedness." Thus, a repentant heart not only avoids self-absorbed penance, but acts on faith to seek wisdom, to be passionately obedient, and to relate to God with the fullness of his or her being.

Yearning for Relationship
Returning to the psalm: After asking for cleansing, the refreshing purity of soul that comes from bathing in God's generous grace, David continues his humble prayer:

> Create in me a clean heart, O God,
> And renew a steadfast spirit within me.
> Do not cast me away from Thy presence,
> And do not take Thy Holy Spirit from me.
> Restore to me the joy of Thy salvation,
> And sustain me with a willing spirit. (verses 10-12)

What strikes me about these verses is the intensity of David's plea and the focus on relationship. The prayer here is succinct and direct, but still gracefully poetic. The poet yearns with the entirety of his being for restoration with God. Not to alleviate guilt, not to feel better about himself, not to manage and control his life, but to know God. The worst punishment the psalmist can imagine is being cut off from God, losing relationship with the One who matters most. When we experience grief over the loss of family and friends, consider how much more our grief should be, but rarely is, over the rift our sin produces with the Father. This is the intense sorrow David communicates here, the threat his sin poses to the deep intimacy he so longs for with his Creator.

David concludes his prayer by citing God's ultimate desire for repentance—restored relationship and total commitment of the heart.

> O Lord, open my lips,
> That my mouth may declare Thy praise.
> For Thou dost not delight in sacrifice, otherwise I would
>   give it;
> Thou art not pleased with burnt offering.
> The sacrifices of God are a broken spirit;
> A broken and a contrite heart, O God, Thou wilt not
>   despise. (verses 15-17)

David desires to worship, to praise his God for His lovingkindness and mercy. Then, despite the fact that he lived under the Law (before Christ's life and sacrifice), David realizes that it's not going through the motions that God desires from us, not simply saying "I'm sorry" and making the appropriate temple sacrifices according to the religious law and custom. God desires *us*. The burnt offerings and sacrifices are only to serve as reminders; they themselves are not the supernatural vehicle of relationship with God, only a symbol of the sacrifice of our pride and selfishness on the altar of our hearts. Our Father desires our broken spirit, our broken and contrite hearts. He wants us fully attuned to our need for Him, to His love for us, to His presence in every moment of our lives. Rather than going through the motions to appease God and feel better ourselves (much like paying a speeding ticket to a stern, uncaring judge), true repentance shatters our heart with the weight of our Abba Father's exceeding love. A broken and contrite heart is awed by God's glorious, perfect standard and humbled by the gift of grace that forgives our sins.

5. Why is recognizing the truth about ourselves and God a significant starting point in our repentance?

6. Does the fact that David remained a "man after God's heart" (Acts 13:22) even though he committed adultery, murder, and deception encourage you, frighten you, unsettle you, delight you? Why?

CONFESSION: A BRIDGE TO HEAVEN

Since then we have a great high priest who has passed through the heavens, Jesus the Son of God, . . . let us therefore draw near with confidence to the throne of grace, that we may receive mercy and may find grace to help in time of need. (Hebrews 4:14,16)

It's simple, old-fashioned even, but not outdated: we confess our sin before God. We come to our senses and leave the pig trough, fully aware of both our grievous offense to the Father and His unquenchable, grace-filled love for us. We ask for His mercy, humbled by our unworthiness before the perfect Creator of the universe, and emboldened by our identity through Christ and through our trust in our Abba's lovingkindness.

Think of yourself as being alone in a small, quiet room. You're aware of how you protect yourself rather than risking loving others as Christ does; of the anger you take out on your spouse; of the loneliness you alleviate through false idols and empty, self-centered relationships—all your various sins float through your stream of consciousness. If you are unwilling to emotionally and physically fall on your face and cry out to God, then you must ask yourself how much you really desire repentance. Do you desire personal change, or do you desire to know intimacy with your Father?

If we have encountered the gospel, then our deepest desire— beneath the struggle of fleshly temptations, the pain of relational struggles, the contempt we pour on ourselves and others, the hateful anger and disappointment we have toward God—is to know and love our Father.

Thus, confession becomes a love letter of humility, sorrow, passion, and hope, not a rote litany that we perceive as magically transforming us into acceptables before God. Rather, when we confess to our Father, we are communicating with Him directly—a process that always benefits us both—and we are reminding ourselves of truth. Confession should lead to worship, to the thrill of relationship with our Abba, to the cleanness of heart and spirit that we saw David speak of in Psalm 51:

> Create in me a clean heart, O God,
> And renew a steadfast spirit within me. . . .
> Restore to me the joy of Thy salvation,
> And sustain me with a willing spirit. (verses 10,12)

Writer Frederick Buechner defines confession this way: "To confess your sins to God is not to tell him anything he doesn't already know. Until you confess them, however, they are the abyss between you. When you confess them, they become the bridge."[1] Expanding his metaphor, we have seen in other chapters how our inherent selfishness, including temptations and addictive/idolatrous tendencies, point out our need for God through Christ. They point to the gap between ourselves and God. However, when we confess out of our brokenness, we traverse our Father's miraculous bridge of grace up to Him. He continuously runs down the path of our return with arms outstretched and eyes brimming with joyful tears.

JOURNALING THE JOURNEY

From My Journal
I can't shake the conversation I had last week with my friend Scott. We were discussing our marriages and lives openly and vulnerably, both disclosing the struggle between our selfishness

and attempting to love our wives like Christ. After I expounded for a while on why I knew I did certain things that hurt Dotti and hindered my relationship with God (one of the dangers of all my counseling experience), Scott stopped me cold with one simple question: "Do you ever fall face down before God and weep for your sins, ask Him for grace, then weep for the joy of His forgiveness?" I was stunned and hung my head. Inside I instantly wanted to shoot back, "Do you?" and deflect his loving rebuke. But I couldn't. Scott was right. So often I spend all this time talking about my sin, thinking through and processing why I do it, how I do it, and what the consequences are, that I gloss over my need for God, for His forgiveness. Scott's words reminded me of another friend's loving charge to me in a similar conversation a few months ago: "You may know about repentance, and can probably write an A-plus paper on it, but you'll never change because of it. You'll never change until you're broken by the weight of your sin and crushed by the mercy of God's grace."

Scott and I ended up praying together and it was rich. The next morning I found myself alone with God and knew that I longed to bow before Him. I realized I can never even attempt to write this book apart from Him and my relationship with Him. I confessed. I worshiped.

For Your Journal

The Book of Common Prayer offers this traditional prayer of confession:

> Most merciful God,
> we confess that we have sinned against you
> in thought, word, and deed,
> by what we have done,
> and by what we have left undone.
> We have not loved you with our whole heart;
> we have not loved our neighbors as ourselves.
> We are truly sorry and we humbly repent.

For the sake of your Son Jesus Christ,
have mercy on us and forgive us;
that we may delight in your will,
and walk in your ways,
to the glory of your Name. Amen.[2]

While this is certainly not a formula, it reminds us of the general categories of our sinfulness: sins of omission, often when we withhold ourselves from others out of self-protection and fear; sins of commission, the overt acts, words, and thoughts that often come to mind first; sins of being, the condition of our selfish, prideful heart that consistently thinks of ourselves first.

Write out this prayer, Psalm 51, or one of your own and reflect on God's truth as reflected in them. Or write a letter or poem to God that expresses your heart's weather at this point. Allow yourself to be as honest as possible before God, confessing your sins, your need of His grace and mercy, and your ultimate longing for intimacy with Him. No one needs to see this journal entry except you and God.

6

EXERCISING
A REPENTANT HEART

As a boy I often visited my ailing grandfather in the nursing home. One Saturday morning I raced ahead of my parents down the ammonia-smelling hallway and into his room. Inside I found a nurse lifting Granddaddy's legs and bending them back; she repeated this several times before she noticed me.

"I'm giving him some exercise," she explained. "Since he's not able to walk and exercise himself, I come every day and stretch his muscles so they don't atrophy."

My ten-year-old mind puzzled over this explanation. "What's atrophy mean?" I asked.

"It's when your muscles or other body parts begin to deteriorate because they're not being used. It's something like your bike; if you don't ride it, eventually it gets all dirty and rusty and breaks down."

The word stuck in my mind like a warning flare, and I've carried it with me to this day. In fact, nowhere does the word *atrophy* seem more applicable than to a repentant heart. While we can never change completely and perfectly until we reach

Heaven, as far as repentance goes, the experience and evidence are indeed in the living-out of it. If we have genuinely faced the crushing weight of our sinful selfishness and felt the paradoxical heavy freedom of grace, then we begin to make different choices about the way we live.

That's not to say that we don't continue to struggle with temptations and choices, that we don't fail from time to time, day by day. However, exercising a repentant heart, avoiding the atrophy of sinful self-centeredness, means a change in being, in lifestyle, choosing to remember the truth about who we are and who God is. It means living out of the still, quiet place inside where the Holy Spirit dwells; it means basing our actions on our heart's truest desire. Rather than sinning cavalierly, cynically, or resignedly, we choose the vertical path to knowing our Father. While sin still pulls us down from time to time, we get right back up and continue on the narrow path. This reminds us that repentance is ongoing, continual, progressive, reflective of our continual need and desire of our Abba's presence, guidance, and love. While we still struggle, our choices to avoid sinning as much as possible and our heartfelt grief and confession when we do, reveal the transcendent glory of our Redeemer. As Martin Luther said, "To do it [sin] no more is the truest repentance."[1]

Obviously Luther is not implying that we can ever be totally without sin, but that choosing to pursue God rather than self is reflected in a steady decrease of sinful choices. While repentance looks different on each of us (more about this later), some general categories apply to all our repentant hearts. These are not formulaic, how-to, checklist kinds of categories, but rather areas that consistently emerge, in Scripture and in believers' lives.

OBEDIENCE: ACTING ON FAITH

As obedient children, do not be conformed to the former lusts which were yours in your ignorance, but like the Holy One who called you, be holy yourselves also in all

your behavior; because it is written, "You shall be holy,
for I am holy." (1 Peter 1:14-16)

The Idolatry of Duty

So often we as Christians tend to make obedience an idol rather
than the fruit of repentant hearts. This is probably due to our ori-
gins. After the fall of Adam and Eve, God revealed Himself
through the Law and asked that those who loved and served Him
adhere to it. Thus, followers of Yahweh found themselves creating
checklists of dos and don'ts in order to maintain the often
demanding and complicated minutiae of the Law. This checklist maintenance quickly became more important than what it
was designed for—relationship with the Creator.

As we know from the New Testament, Christ came to fulfill
the requirements of the Law for all sinners, once and for all.
"There is therefore now no condemnation for those who are in
Christ Jesus. For the law of the Spirit of life in Christ Jesus has
set you free from the law of sin and of death" (Romans 8:1-2).
However, as Christ experienced in His lifetime, the keepers of the
Jewish faith had evolved into legalists and hypocrites. The Pharisees and other religious leaders kept the letter of the Law and
maintained self-righteous public personas, but did not relate with
the Father at all in their hearts. Christ repeatedly denounced this
facade of faith: "Woe to you, scribes and Pharisees, hypocrites!
For you clean the outside of the cup and of the dish, but inside
they are full of robbery and self-indulgence. You blind Pharisee,
first clean the inside of the cup and of the dish, so that the outside of it may become clean also" (Matthew 23:25-26).

In fact, in our time the term *pharisee* has become synony-
mous with hypocrite or legalist. While we often nod in agreement when we read about Pharisees in the gospels or spot dis-
crepancies in others' lives, we rarely examine our own motives
for obedience. In our Christian culture today, sadly, many believers obey out of duty, obligation, or merit. They either go through
the motions of what they think God requires of them, hoping this
will get them by, while inwardly dying, cut off from their Father;

or they obey out of the hope that they can "win" God's favor with their good behavior. We see this evidenced by many of the believers who claim a trouble-free life of health, wealth, and prosperity as long as they obey. This is simply not true. If we obey out of duty ("That's what Christians are supposed to do," one counselee once told me) or out of a false merit system (which we can never fulfill), we fail to obey out of love for our Father, out of the repentant heart that longs to know Him above all else.

Obeying for Relationship
When we focus on obeying because of the relationship we have, the actual choices of obedience become secondary. We become less concerned with having a quiet time in prayer and Bible study for its own sake, to check off our daily list and thus feel good about ourselves. Instead we become hungry for time with our Abba Father, whether to cry out a love-hymn in joyful praise or our deepest pains and fears in a lament. We long for communication with Him, for intimacy in the deepest core of our being. We desire to read His Word with the fervor of a child longing to hear a bedtime story, rather than with dispassionate, exegetical scrutiny.

Will there be times when we don't feel like reading our Bible or praying? Should we be consistent in these and other spiritual disciplines anyway? Of course. We should not be dictated to by our whims, moods, and emotions. But (and this is a crucial but), we must not ignore these feelings and attempt to cut them off from who we are before our Lord. He wants our heart, all of it, the entire spectrum of internal weather that we're capable of feeling, not a rote obedience that's internally disconnected. Discipline and obedience should remind us of Him and what we desire the most; they should bring us closer to what we feel about our lives and about God (even the feelings "good" Christians often don't allow themselves—fear, anger, jealousy, disappointment, doubt).

The Risk of Faith
This brings us to why it's often so much easier to obey routinely, dispassionately rather than with the full force of our heart:

obedience requires acting on faith. Obedience in some ways testifies to faith, "the assurance of things hoped for, the conviction of things not seen" (Hebrews 11:1). Obeying out of a repentant heart causes much more suffering than simply going through the motions trying to change for its own sake.

Recall Steve, our family man who feels addicted to pornography. In regard to the obedience required to combat addictions and temptations, Steve states, "Being faithful in the small things—like resisting daily temptations—feels so futile. As long as I can keep my sin hidden from my family and pretend there are no consequences, why not give in to temptation?" By refusing to even fight temptation, Steve refuses to hope in things presently unseen. In other words, he refuses to act on faith, the hope that God does love and care about him and his needs and desires. The instant gratification of self often blinds us, as it does Steve, to the desire we have of hoping in God. Such hope usually requires that we wait patiently. This is, of course, antithetical to our microwave society's message of instant fulfillment. But true faith requires us to fight the good fight, even if we fail sometimes, in order to hope more deeply in our Father and to long more fully for relationship with Him.

Steve's weak faith and negative view of obedience thus illuminate the rest of his statement: "So if the daily faith-struggles feel futile, then the big ones—like trusting God about my job, my marriage, or my son's operation—feel impossible." Such a perspective parallels the servant's justification of faithlessness in the parable of the talents. In this story Jesus compares the Kingdom of God and how we relate to the Father to a man going on a long trip who delegates his finances to his servants while he's away. He gives one five thousand dollars, another two thousand, and the third one thousand. The first two servants invest the money and double it. The third servant, on the other hand, buries his sum in the ground.

When the man returns and asks about his investments, the first two servants report their dividends and receive their master's blessing—"Well done, good and faithful slave; you were faithful with a few things, I will put you in charge of many things; enter into the joy of your master" (Matthew 25:23). However, the third servant attempts to justify his hyper-conservative stewardship:

> "Master, I know you have high standards and hate careless ways, that you demand the best and make no allowances for error. I was afraid I might disappoint you, so I found a good hiding place and secured your money. Here it is, safe and sound down to the last cent."
>
> The master was furious. "That's a terrible way to live! It's criminal to live cautiously like that! If you knew I was after the best, why did you do less than the least? The least you could have done would have been to invest the sum with the bankers, where at least I would have gotten a little interest.
>
> "Take the thousand and give it to the one who risked the most. And get rid of this 'play-it-safe' who won't go out on a limb. Throw him out into utter darkness." (Matthew 25:24-30, MESSAGE)

Perhaps the punishment seems too harsh, in our judgment, for the "crime." But this makes Jesus' point all the more: obedience requires acting on faith, which always involves risk. This doesn't mean we should place our savings accounts on a Las Vegas roulette wheel. But metaphorically, we do indeed need to risk high stakes (often our own comfort, convenience, security, and control) with our actions of faith. We must be willing to wait patiently on the Lord (Psalm 27:14, 40:1-2) and consistently take the risk to obey Him in the meantime, even when we don't feel like it, even when our "rational" faculties remind us of the frustration in not seeing or feeling God's presence. Our Father, so it seems in the parable, wants us to bet all of ourselves on knowing Him.

This is exactly what He has done to know us: subject a living part of Himself, His only Son, to the full wrath that we deserve. God, in essence, gambled the only Innocent Man to purchase the rest of us. His gift of free will only reinforces this gamble since we can choose not to accept this unfathomable gift or to embrace it. Such high stakes, indeed, serve as an incredible example of the kind of faith, and subsequent obedience, God desires from us.

According to Eugene Peterson, such risk-filled obedience emerges out of two main ingredients—remembering God's faithfulness in the past and hoping faithfully (believing) in His promises for the future.

> We need roots in the past to give obedience ballast and breadth; we need a vision of the future to give obedience direction and goal. And they must be connected. There must be organic unity between them. If we never learn how to do this, extend the boundaries of our lives beyond the dates enclosed by our birth and death and acquire an understanding of God's way as something larger and more complete than the anecdotes in our private diaries, we will forever be missing the point of things.[2]

Such a perspective, one that eagerly seeks the larger mural of God's design and not the narrow, minuscule snapshot of our own immediate experience and self-interest, undergirds the obedience of a repentant heart.

1. What comes to mind when you think of "obedience"?
2. Would you describe your Christian journey so far as characterized more by duty or passion? What makes the difference?
3. What does it mean for you to be a faithful (obedient) steward with "the smaller things"?

LOVING OTHERS AS OURSELVES

Not only does a repentant heart produce the fruit of obedience, it also continually attempts to love others well. In fact, the primary commands of Christ, following "love the Lord your God with all your heart, and with all your soul, and with all your mind" (Matthew 22:37), refer to loving others. "A new commandment I give to you, that you love one another, even as I have loved you, that you also love one another" (John 13:34).

Suffering

Such love, like repentance itself, does not come naturally. As I watch my toddler daughter play with other children and scream rather than share her toy telephone, it saddens me to witness the intrinsic selfishness within my heart, and all of our hearts, as well. But thanks to the power of our Father's love and the process of spiritual growth rooted in our redeemed hearts, we are called to love others with the selfless, supernatural love of Christ.

Whether this is a new concept for you or a worn cliché from your first Sunday school class, loving others remains one of the fundamental challenges of faith. *It requires suffering.* And most of us are committed to avoiding suffering. So choosing to love others requires us to risk, out of obedience, the same kind of love, compassion, and grace our Father risks with us. The return is not guaranteed, and if we are calculating or anticipating others' responses to our love then it likely isn't love at all, but more likely manipulation, self-centeredness, and the idolatry of control.

What does it mean to love others out of a repentant heart? While countless books and volumes address that question, some very well and some not so very well, here I would remind you of two important thoughts: loving others can never be reduced to a formula; and the extent we're capable of loving others reflects our experience with the Father's gift of grace over the sorrow of our own failures.

This first thought is consistent with the theme of this book: that repentance itself cannot be formulaic, but neither is it a subjective, nebulous abstract malleable to any personal definition. Similarly, each of us might have a different view of loving others more than ourselves. Some of us need to confront others more often with bold, humble words and actions that might not be received well. Others need to be consistently kinder and more thoughtful to those around us. All of us are called to both since they both reflect Jesus' law of love to us.

Hard Words

How do we know when to lovingly speak hard words and when to graciously offer kindness? So much of loving others with Christ's love depends upon the context of the relationship. Christ expressed angry criticism toward the Pharisees for their selfish hypocrisy; He even raged and cleared out the moneychangers in the Temple. Nonetheless, He was loving each group well.

Before you make a list of folks you can't wait to blast for their hypocrisy, sinful lifestyles, or personal affronts, you must also consider a crucial caveat:

> "Do not judge lest you be judged. For in the way you judge, you will be judged; and by your standard of measure, it will be measured to you. And why do you look at the speck that is in your brother's eye, but do not notice the log that is in your own eye? Or how can you say to your brother, 'Let me take the speck out of your eye,' and behold, the log is in your own eye? You hypocrite, first take the log out of your own eye, and then you will see clearly to take the speck out of your brother's eye." (Matthew 7:1-5)

Eugene Peterson paraphrases this passage in contemporary language:

> "Don't pick on people, jump on their failures, criticize their faults—unless, of course, you want the same treatment. That critical spirit has a way of boomeranging. It's easy to see a smudge on your neighbor's face and be oblivious to the ugly sneer on your own. Do you have the nerve to say, 'Let me wash your face for you,' when your own face is distorted by contempt?" (Matthew 7:1-4, MESSAGE)

We must be willing to examine our hearts and our motives for traces of self-centeredness, revenge and retaliation (how many "loving confrontations" amount to nothing more than petty revenge?), and self-righteousness. Before we can even begin to say hard words out of "love" to others, we must first say harder words to ourselves. We must pray and seek the Spirit's guidance. We must never assume the power to judge.

If after we pray and examine our motives we still believe that loving someone requires hard words, then we should share honestly and directly. This often means risking that person's acceptance of us; it may jeopardize the entire relationship. But the law of Christ's love requires this kind of penetrating, bold love that cares more for a person's relationship with our shared Father than whether or not that person will continue to like us.

Kindness

On the other hand, much of loving others means thinking of others before self, giving them what you yourself long for (from the previous point—consider that ultimately we do long for accountability and lovingly dispensed hard words from others to challenge us to our commitment to Christ). Acts of kindness, courtesy, respect, and gratitude go a long way in touching others, providing them with a drink of Life-giving Water.

A good friend once told me that during a life-threatening bout with depression the one thing that kept her going, the one thing she came to count on for comfort each day, was the kindness of the waitress at the diner where she ate lunch daily. My friend always sat in the same booth and her waitress treated her with such kindness in the mundane acts of pouring coffee and serving a sandwich that my friend would get tears in her eyes. She credits God's love through this waitress as literally keeping her alive. Did the waitress have any idea that she affected my friend this way? Probably not.

While this is a dramatic example, think for a moment how you are affected when you come home after an excruciating day of flat tires, sick kids, late projects, and traffic snarls to see the tender smile on your spouse's face. Or a friend's phone call, for no particular reason. Or an encouraging note, unexpected gift, or shared meal. As human beings we all crave relationship, even though we've all been hurt consistently and consequently protect ourselves from other people. Loving others with kindness means a thoughtfulness, a sensitivity to the needs and longings of others that seeks no dividend for itself. As Jesus puts it in His Sermon on the Mount (in fact, following the above passage on log-speck hypocrisy): "Here is a simple, rule-of-thumb guide for behavior: Ask yourself what you want people to do for you, then grab the initiative and do it for *them*. Add up God's Law and Prophets and this is what you get" (Matthew 7:12, MESSAGE).

How do we know when to show love and kindness? Without becoming a legalistic formula in itself (to feel good about oneself), the answer is *always*. Since we are inherently selfish, seeking to love others with the love of our Father is always in order. Obviously, this requires tasting the Father's love in the first place, embracing the humbling gift of grace He mercifully extends to us.

4. What pictures pop into your mind when you consider loving others as yourself? What does this love look like on a daily basis?

FORGIVING OTHERS

Never is love harder than in forgiving others of their offenses to us. This is, in fact, one of the most significant ways to love others more than ourselves. What does this mean? A quick "I forgive you" or "forgive and forget"? No, we can't reduce forgiveness of others to an easy how-to; it requires our very own experiential knowledge of our Father's love and mercy.

Jesus addresses this very question from one of His disciples. "Then Peter came and said to Him, 'Lord, how often shall my brother sin against me and I forgive him? Up to seven times?' Jesus said to him, 'I do not say to you, up to seven times, but up to seventy times seven'" (Matthew 18:21-22). In other words, throw the formula out the window and forgive your brother or sister always, daily.

Jesus follows this up with the parable of the wicked slave who begs forgiveness on a huge debt from his master but then refuses to extend grace on a small debt owed him by another. The master then demands exact payment from the wicked servant since he would not show grace to his own borrower. The message comes through loud and clear: "So shall My heavenly Father also do to you, if each of you does not forgive his brother from your heart" (Matthew 18:35).

This message also arises in Jesus' instruction on how to pray. One petition of the Lord's Prayer (Matthew 6:9-13) tells us to ask God's forgiveness and reminds us to keep forgiving others. The traditional translation, "Forgive us our debts, as we also have forgiven our debtors," is often interpreted as meaning that God forgives us in direct proportion to how much we forgive others. While the two channels of forgiveness have a corollary relationship, this interpretation is flawed logically as well as theologically. Writer Frederick Buechner explains:

> In the first place, forgiveness that's conditional isn't
> really forgiveness at all, just Fair Warning, and in the
> second place our unforgivingness is among those things
> about us which we need to have God forgive us most.
> What Jesus is apparently saying is that the pride which
> keeps us from forgiving is the same pride which keeps
> us from accepting forgiveness, and will God please help
> us do something about it.[3]

Such confession of this prideful difficulty in forgiving others humbles us and forces us to remember what is true about ourselves and our Father. Like the master in Jesus' parable, God has forgiven us an unfathomable debt that we could never pay. Both the weight of the debt and the gift of its fulfillment should shatter our petty grudges and the deep bitterness we tend to harbor against others. Tasting the nectar of such grace should move our hearts, soften our sense of justice, to the point where we eagerly and earnestly forgive others. This doesn't mean forgetting the offense or pretending that it never happened, but simply loving them with the grace of the prodigal's father when there's no logical reason to. In fact, loving others is rarely logical because we will consistently get hurt. (We will examine more about loving others in the next chapter.)

Exercising a repentant heart also means asking others to forgive you as you become aware of your harm to them. While there is again no rule for when to tell others you've offended them (they may not even be aware of being sinned against), often the Holy Spirit, as well as the general guidelines evident in Scripture, cue our hearts. This requires relinquishing our pride, seeking forgiveness before the Father, and humbling ourselves before those we've hurt through our sinfulness. This might mean apologizing for a rash indictment or subtle barb, or making restitution if material goods are involved. While the grievance cannot be undone, if there are ways to restore some of what has been damaged by your gossip, theft, lies, or whatever, then seek to do so out of a loving concern for those you've harmed. Restitution should never be used as a bribe to demand the other's forgiveness, nor should it attempt to erase the damage done. It should be a love offering flowing from your desire to restore relationship with the person because of the ultimate relationship you have with God.

5. How would you describe the relationship between your own experience of forgiveness from God and the forgiveness you extend to others?
6. How does requesting someone else's forgiveness demonstrate your love for that person?

FRUIT OF THE SPIRIT

But I say, walk by the Spirit, and you will not carry out the desire of the flesh. For the flesh sets its desire against

the Spirit, and the Spirit against the flesh; for these are in
opposition to one another, so that you may not do the
things that you please. But if you are led by the Spirit,
you are not under the Law. (Galatians 5:16-18)

I believe walking by the Spirit is another way to say exercising
a repentant heart. In fact, the heart of the Christian life, which
most of us learn early by experience, is that no matter how much
we improve ourselves through discipline, memorizing Scripture,
counseling, reading good books, or attending seminars, we'll
never be transformed until we give up our schemes for self-
improvement and let the Holy Spirit work on us. That's not to
undermine the benefits of the aforementioned aids, and especially not to underestimate the essential requirements of our heart
attitude and subsequent obedience. But much of the work of
repentance is simply allowing the Spirit to lead, shape, whisper,
and kindle sparks of yearning for our Abba Father. Indeed, it is
the Spirit who enables us to approach God as our "Daddy," as
adopted sons and daughters, heirs with Christ. "For you have
not received a spirit of slavery leading to fear again . . . . The
Spirit Himself bears witness with our spirit that we are children
of God" (Romans 8:15-16).

Frederick Buechner describes the Holy Spirit as the member
of the Trinity who is "the mystery within us." This often bothers
us as we struggle with what it means to live a life of faith out of
our repentant hearts. This reminds us once again of how easily
we slip into resisting this mystery, which necessitates relinquishing control, by becoming managers with spiritual checklists. Too often, we'd rather have something we can do, control,
perform, try harder at, than seek God's Spirit, trust, and relax.
However, exercising a repentant heart requires that we let go
and explore the mystery of what it means to have the Holy Spirit
living inside us, changing us, conforming us to the likeness of
Jesus. The Spirit's role in our Christian journeys cannot be under-
estimated.

So what does it mean to embrace this "mystery within us"

and allow Him to move us vertically toward the Father? In Galatians 5:25 Paul defines it as an internal process ("If we live by the Spirit"—because the Spirit dwells in us, in our hearts) expressed through an external metaphor ("let us also walk by the Spirit"). Such a radical internal shift produces an external one as well. Living and walking become inextricable expressions of our new identities in Christ. Paul's words concisely and wonderfully communicate the indivisible union of our part with God's part.

They also remind us of both extremes: practicing legalism and spiritual management on one hand and waiting passively for that "cosmic zap" on the other. Neither method produces change or represents repentance accurately and fully. We're required to do our part, which often means discovering our part each day, within the confines of obedience to Christ. While mystical visions or mysterious, ineffable moods may descend on us from the Spirit, we should not make our lives and spiritual pursuits contingent upon them. We can't "force" the Holy Spirit to change us the way we want to; however, living passively and cautiously, waiting for a felt mystical experience or a visible sign, will frustrate and paralyze us just as much as relying on our own efforts. The mysterious journey of faith lies in between, requiring us to be constantly relying on the Spirit, continually relating with our Father. A repentant heart depends on the Father in every aspect of life, including when we fail. And even though we can't always see or discern the Spirit's enabling power, it's incredible comfort to know He's there, allowing us to love others and attest to God's goodness, despite our own struggles and sinfulness.

7. Try to describe your understanding of the Holy Spirit based on what you've experienced. How does your description or definition compare with what you've been taught about the Spirit?

A SHARP CONTRAST

It is obvious what kind of life develops out of trying to
get your own way all the time: repetitive, loveless, cheap
sex; a stinking accumulation of mental and emotional
garbage; frenzied and joyless grabs for happiness; trinket
gods; magic-show religion; paranoid loneliness; cut-
throat competition; all-consuming-yet-never-satisfied
wants; a brutal temper; an impotence to love or be loved;
divided homes and divided lives; small-minded and lop-
sided pursuits; the vicious habit of depersonalizing
everyone into a rival; uncontrolled and uncontrollable
addictions; ugly parodies of community. I could go on.
(Galatians 5:19-21, MESSAGE)

Sound familiar? As I reviewed the Galatians passage on the fruit of
the flesh and the fruit of the Spirit, I found I practically knew it by
heart. I recalled a youth musical I participated in at the small church
where I grew up many years ago. The musical had a wonderful
pop beat with scriptural lyrics, and that's what darted through my
mind as I thought of this passage. There was nothing wrong with
that youth musical, and I'm sure many heard the gospel message
through it. But what I did with it amounted to turning Scripture
into jingles. Thus, when I think about "Now the deeds of the flesh
are evident, which are: immorality, impurity, sensuality, idolatry, sor-
cery, enmities, strife, jealousy, outbursts of anger, disputes, dis-
sensions, factions, envying, drunkenness, carousing . . ." it becomes
an abstract warning list veneered with a pop melody. However,
when I read a modern paraphrase like Eugene Peterson's, I'm suddenly jolted by each one's applicability to my life.

My point is not that I prefer a modern paraphrase over a traditional translation, but rather how often we lose sight of the
personal conviction of Scripture because we callous ourselves
to words that become little more than concepts. I can't read this
passage and not be convicted, and regardless of your Scripture
preference, I hope you can't either.

While these selfish feelings, thoughts, and acts might plague us, we choose not to pursue them as false idols. They serve self and, as we covered in chapter 3, the altar of our hearts can only be satisfied knowing God. When we choose our own voice over the voice of the Spirit, these "fruits" collect beneath us like bruised, moldy peaches, rotten before they even hit the ground.

> What happens when we live God's way? He brings gifts into our lives, much the same way that fruit appears in an orchard—things like affection for others, exuberance about life, serenity. We develop a willingness to stick with things, a sense of compassion in the heart, and a conviction that a basic holiness permeates things and people. We find ourselves involved in loyal commitments, not needing to force our way in life, able to marshal and direct our energies wisely. (Galatians 5:22-24, MESSAGE)

Unfortunately, many times we feel pressured, not encouraged, by Paul's list of spiritual fruits. Instead of realizing that these are the wonderful byproducts of living in the Spirit, we often try to live out these fruits first. But this reversal will not work: producing the appearance of good works does not increase our reliance on the Holy Spirit. To the contrary, we're right back in the vicious cycle of self-reliance.

Instead we should find hope, encouragement, and vision. This list of sweet fruit, in sharp contrast to the list of rotting, fleshly produce, gives us clear ideas of how we should be acting based on the internal process of repentance and redemption taking place in our very beings. If we're seeking the Lord, relying on the Spirit, obeying passionately, loving graciously, and hoping fervently, then these fruits will blossom and ripen. This picture is of Christ Himself, a vision of who we long to be, who we are becoming. This is, in fact, the very essence of repentance: "True repentance spends less time looking at the past and saying, 'I'm sorry,' than to the future and saying, 'Wow!'"[4]

When we consider ourselves within the context of Paul's "fruit list," our mouths should hang open in a wide *O* of joyful, hopeful amazement. This "wow" is a glimpse of Heaven, of who our Father has created us to be and is perfecting us to be. This offers tremendous hope in the midst of the suffering necessitated by our sinful world. This hope of Heaven reminds us of the great joy ahead, the great fulfillment of creation through the redemptive power of Christ and the will of the Father. With such a hope set before us, passionate obedience, loving others, forgiving them, and producing fruit of the Spirit become not about us, not about spiritual improvement or cosmetic changes of behavior, but about love. It draws us to praise and worship, to rejoicing what we taste now, and longing for what is to come.

JOURNALING THE JOURNEY

From My Journal
I can't find words to write today—too restless. I feel like I'm on the verge of something, but what? It feels like I'm almost on the verge of freedom, of peace, of settledness. What am I afraid of?

I think there's something in me that really does want to write this book on repentance, that really does believe I can say something about it, about the process of knowing God, about His goodness. I believe I really do want to write another novel and just give myself to both of them, to the writing, to God's pleasure being allowed to shine through the very process of writing, and I fight that. I make it laborious and angry; I have to write. No, I love to write, it's a privilege to write, I've won a kind of lottery in being called and allowed to write. And I love it. But it also scares the heck out of me. What if I put my heart into the repentance book and really feel that it's the best I can do (at this point in my life, at least) and it's ill-received and flops. What will sustain me to write? Is writing a matter of obedience for me? Ironically, writing a book on repentance is repentance for me, being disciplined about my swimming regimen in an ocean of grace.

For Your Journal

What do you long for in your relationship with God? What holds you back? What picture do you have before you (of yourself, of Him, of others) that spurs you on to knowing Him?

7

COMMUNITY AND ACCOUNTABILITY

—

Steve nervously knocked on his friend Dan's door. Steve had called with an urgency and vulnerability Dan had never heard before, and he eagerly agreed to meet with Steve that evening. As the two walked the trail through the nearby evergreen park, Steve finally plunged in.

"I—I need your help, Dan. I'm struggling like crazy. I've been buying pornography; I feel addicted to my fantasy life. I don't know what to do. I've tried and tried to give it up by myself, but I realized last night at church that I need to share this with someone I trust, someone who can hold me accountable and help me overcome temptations. Someone who can help me decide how to handle this with my wife." He was out of breath and looked over at his friend.

Dan paused but finally responded, "You're my friend, Steve. Why, we've been friends since college. You know you can trust me. I'm honored that you felt like you could call on me. I'll help any way I can."

Steve was visibly relieved. "When Anne and I were first married and I found that I still struggled with old habits, I called up our pastor and made an appointment. It was so awkward, like the man had never had a sexual feeling or temptation in his life. After I finished sharing, he said, 'Well, Steve, you know the problem, and we both know Jesus is the solution, so why do you think you're still struggling? Have you been memorizing Scripture and saying it aloud during times of temptation? Have you been having a regular prayer time? What about service? Getting actively involved in ministry doesn't leave much time for us to allow Satan into our imagination.'"

Dan stopped on the footpath and turned to Steve. "You've got to be kidding! Good grief, there's some truth in what he's saying, but that totally ignores what's going on in your heart between you and God. That makes me angry . . . and sad."

Steve couldn't believe his friend's compassion and empathy. He felt his burden lighten a little more. "Yeah, I only went back once for a follow-up 'accountability' meeting. It only made me feel worse, more guilty and secretive, more alone, like I'm the only man who ever struggles with his sexuality."

Dan laughed out loud. "No way. I struggle in many of the same ways you do. In fact, I used to feel exactly the same way—isolated, afraid. But then I began to meet together with a group of men for a breakfast and Bible study once a week. I finally began to trust them, and we opened up to one another. It's made a huge difference in my faith walk, knowing other men care and walk alongside me. That's what I want to do with you."

Steve looked away, watched the last shimmers of sunlight weave across the horizon. He felt tears well up in his eyes for the first time in a long time.

Michelle sat quietly and sipped her coffee. She had arranged this time alone with her husband with a specific discussion in mind, but now she wasn't sure how to begin. Brian waited patiently on the sofa next to her. She had rehearsed it in her mind a thousand times, but she still wasn't sure how her husband would respond. She couldn't shake the fear that he would humiliate her, saying, "I told you so. It's about time you listened."

She began softly, "I've been thinking and praying, honey, and I think you're right that I do too much. I stay so busy and so committed to church and school events that I don't have much left over to give you and the kids. I want to change." Michelle fought back tears. "I want to be different. I know this isn't what God wants of me."

Brian nodded and scooted close to her, pulling her into his arms. Joy leaped inside; he couldn't believe what he was hearing. He knew Michelle could be such a different woman—a more relaxed, warm, spontaneous, and carefree woman—from the one he'd grown accustomed to, the one who rigidly followed her daytimer as if it were a presidential planner.

"I know; it's okay. I'll help you as best I can," Brian whispered. "I love you. This isn't just about you, it's about both of us. I want to love you, really love you." His wife softened in his arms.

"You already have. You've refused to let me detach from God, and you, by staying busy all the time. You've challenged me to focus on Him first, on loving the people who are most important to me as best I can first, and then giving to others. I want you to keep on helping point out when I'm doing too much. I hope I won't bite your head off like I have before. I'm scared of letting you down, but I'm committed to you."

"You will let me down and I'll let you down. That's what forgiveness and love are all about. That's what marriage, the Church, and the body of believers are all about. Loving each other a little closer toward God."

Joanne couldn't believe what she was doing: dialing Mary, the pastor's wife, to schedule a lunch appointment. She'd wrestled with her guilt, fear, and shame long enough, she decided. It was time to take action.

Mary agreed to meet her the next day and seemed delighted that Joanne would want to spend time with her. After they both ordered the chicken pasta, Joanne felt a yearning inside, an odd kinship, the same feeling she experienced when she missed the deep, intimate friendships she'd had before moving. It was the longing that kept her gossiping with the "in-group" in her singles class, just to have others to be with. Her longing quickly melted into fear: What if Mary was someone she actually liked, what if she'd blown any chance at a friendship with Mary before it even began? After the small talk subsided, Joanne decided to be blunt and get on with her agenda.

"Before we talk any more, I need to tell you why I asked you here. I have a confession to make, a horrible one. And sitting here with you just now makes me realize how much I like you, how I've never even taken a chance to get to know you. I've only relied on hearsay and gossip about what you're really like. And with you being married and a stay-at-home mom, I figured we'd have nothing in common." She paused and sipped her water. Mary's eyes hadn't left hers since she began. "Mary, I've been gossiping about you with some others in the singles department. Just last week someone saw you come out of the liquor store across town and so we've all been exaggerating, saying you probably have a secret drinking problem."

Mary chortled. "Joanne, you're kidding me . . . aren't you? Well, I see that you're not. I appreciate your confession, but why are you telling me this?"

Joanne felt her poised facade caving in. "Oh, Mary, I'm so sorry, I hate what I've been doing. It's wrong, so very wrong, and because I'm so lonely and so afraid of not having any friends, I simply go along with the flow. That's not an excuse at all. I hate what I've done to you. I pray that you'll forgive me."

Mary refolded her napkin in her lap and tried to think of what to say.

Joanne leaned forward. "If you want to leave now, I understand; just know how truly sorry I am. I've already called the women to whom I usually spread the rumors and told them that they're not true. I'm so sorry." Tears sprang from her eyes and her vision blurred to where she couldn't see the expression on Mary's face.

Mary leaned toward the young woman who had fallen apart across from her. When she spoke her voice was surprisingly tender: "Joanne, I forgive you. It's okay, really. I've heard those rumors before and they do hurt me. I feel just as alone and afraid as you do. I've wanted to call and get to know you but been afraid that I had already been judged by everyone. Thank you so much for your courage, for loving our Father enough to face me. Know that you're forgiven. I really want to be your friend."

What do you feel as you read about our imaginary friends and their individual scenarios? Are these scenes too "perfect," even unrealistic? Have you experienced similar times of holy intimacy with others as you've shared the burdens and struggles of your heart?

You'll recall from the last chapter that Jesus commands us to love one another, to exercise our repentant hearts by thinking of others before ourselves, loving them with bold confrontations that point them back to the Father, loving them with kindness and encouragement, forgiving them when they hurt us, asking for forgiveness when we hurt them. While the dynamics of repentance take place largely within us through the Holy Spirit, the results of our sorrow over sinning and our embrace of grace manifest themselves best in relationships. We live out our changed nature by the way we speak, think, and act with those around us—spouses, children, friends, coworkers, parents, our church family, even strangers. The fruit of the Spirit reveals itself best when we love others well.

Since we are relational beings, just as our Creator is a relational being (even within Himself as the Trinity), *living out of a repentant heart means acknowledging and committing to relationships*. From this we then find freedom to love one another through accountability, one of the most misunderstood and misused relational gifts in Christian communities.

1. Have you ever experienced someone like Steve's pastor who remained distant from your struggles and instead offered simplistic advice? How did you feel? How did it affect your faith?
2. Who do you trust implicitly (that is, you could go to them with any sin, any struggle, and know that they would still love you)?

COMMUNITY: PILGRIMS IN PROCESS

Community usually encompasses different spheres of relationships. At the core, there's us and God. Then come those closest to us: our spouse, children, parents, siblings, best friends. Next might be extended family and other friends, followed by coworkers, social acquaintances, professional colleagues, and on and on.

Christians often like to think of the local church as their community and limit their relational pool exclusively to it. For our purposes here, I define community as encompassing both believing and nonbelieving relationships, where we consistently interact the most. I believe a strong community, one that reflects our Father and His perfect relational Trinity, characterizes itself by three traits: (1) room to struggle, a rich soil for doubt, anger, joy, fear, and the whole spectrum of human experiences; (2) a challenge to seek God faithfully and consistently amidst the rushing rapids of our emotions, circumstances, and struggles; and (3) the supernatural, empowering love of Christ. Such a community remembers that we are all pilgrims in process, journeying toward what it means to know, love, and serve the Father, toward becoming more Christlike.

Ideally, the Church would shine with these traits and pierce the surrounding darkness of our fallen world, and many churches do. As most of us know, however, the local church often feels like a trophy gallery of pretend-perfect Christians rather than a body of sinners struggling to know their Father better. Sadly enough, many Christians often trust and confide in their nonbelieving friends more than other Christians because they know they will be allowed to struggle without receiving pat answers or self-righteous judgment.

What limits churches from being the rich body of believers God intends them to be? We'll examine this momentarily, but for now consider that God does not limit Himself to the Church as an exclusive relational vehicle, and as you read through this chapter and consider your own community, do not limit yourself to recalling either the satisfaction of rich community that many churches offer or the aching disappointment where they fail. Consider instead the full spectrum of people you know, love, and relate with.

With these folks and ourselves in mind, let's reconsider Jesus' command to love one another and examine the three traits strong communities exhibit. As you'll recall from last chapter, after loving God with all our being, our next command is to love one another as Christ loves us: "By this all men will know that you are My disciples, if you have love for one another" (John 13:35). The Apostle Paul also stresses the essential importance of our loving one another: "For you were called to freedom, brethren; only do not turn your freedom into an opportunity for the flesh, but through love serve one another. For the whole Law is fulfilled in one word, in the statement, 'You shall love your neighbor as yourself'" (Galatians 5:13-14).

Unfortunately, these commands often remain lofty ideals rather than practical instructions. Relationships, even among Christians (sometimes more so), are messy. We get hurt. We hurt other people. Subtle putdowns, cynical jokes, silent rejections pile up and we often feel like withdrawing from the human race. And perhaps we would withdraw permanently or become totally cynical and selfish, if not for the supernatural love of Christ empowering us through the Holy Spirit. Through this love that we experience, we become willing to love through suffering, and although it's no less painful, it reminds us and others of how our Father loves us.

ROOM TO STRUGGLE: SHARING HONESTLY

This notion that community requires relational suffering is foundational to the first trait of a godly community. We must allow ourselves to struggle and to share who we are and what's going on in our lives out of that struggle. We should allow ourselves to hope and long for relationships that would share some of our burden without taking it away. While other people cannot fill the void inside us where we meet God, they can share our "growing pains." When we try to make relationships into idols, community and any allowance of genuine struggle is violated.

This doesn't mean that we shouldn't long for encouragement, comfort, security, and fellowship from other people, but simply that if we rely on them for who we are, for what we worship, then we're idolaters. Sharing our struggles with others as well as letting them share their struggles with us requires honesty, faith, and love. Because of who our Father is, we can honestly express the pain, discomfort, and agony of our soul. Consider Job, Jeremiah, and Christ Himself as models of what it means to suffer and embrace that suffering, rather than minimizing or denying it. We should allow ourselves to cry, rage, and doubt in front of those we trust and care about. And we should be discreet, for at least two reasons: the timing is not always appropriate (while called to authenticity, we are still called to selflessness—it would be incredibly selfish to ignore a friend's emotions and circumstances just to inconsiderately "share" our own), and the context of the relationship may not be appropriate. We should be willing to be sensitive to others and their struggles and not always look for someone to dump our emotions on. We should respect their time and share gradually, naturally, instead of trying to force or contrive a false sense of trust and intimacy.

One of the most common excuses for not struggling genuinely with others is that there's no one we can trust. While the risk of vulnerability, even rejection, always remains (even in the best and longest relationships), this excuse must not stop us from seeking out others to share our lives with. We should seek out people we can trust, and while we still may feel terrified and afraid of their response, we need to risk, to give them the opportunity to demonstrate Christ to us. Will we be hurt? Will others disappoint us, lecture us insensitively, reject us, and offer trite "spiritual" answers? Of course. But we also will be surprised at times, loved well, encouraged, bolstered in our faith, rebuked lovingly, and drawn closer to our Abba. We should all have people with whom we pretend about nothing.

How should we respond when others take such risks with us? With boldness, honesty, grace, and the love of Christ. Think about what you long for, deep down, beneath the layers of self-contempt, isolation, fear of others, and the multitude of other excuses we find for not sharing genuinely with others. Take a moment and jot these longings down.

While individual lists will vary, I think most lists will, bottom line, reflect two desires: We want to be known fully, seen completely in the total wretchedness of our sin, depravity, and harm to others; and we want to be loved supernaturally in the midst of such a mess. While my counseling experience is somewhat limited, what I experienced with virtually every client was a variation of those two themes. Despite the denial, the pretending, the anger and shame, they wanted me to uncover their worst selves. And then they wanted me to show them some hope by loving them with the Father's love. They want grace; we all want grace.

Consider a client I'll call Ed who came to see me for homosexual struggles. A single man in his early thirties, Ed, tall and handsome, appeared as masculine and rugged as a lumberjack. Inside, however, he struggled with feelings of inferiority, insecurity, and inadequacy in his manhood. He found himself longing for physical relationships with other men and consequently had started seeking out anonymous sexual encounters with them. He hated himself for it, longed to be a better Christian, but didn't know what to do. He wanted a richer and deeper relationship with God but couldn't shake his desires for other men.

While the issue of homosexuality is indeed too complex to go into here, one strategy I followed with Ed was encouraging him to explore the feelings intermeshed in his sexual struggle without yielding to temptation. After several months of slow, gradual progress (Ed began suffering his longings without resorting to acting out; he was becoming aware of what he ultimately longed for), Ed came into my office and announced, "I blew it. I acted out with another man. We're right back where we started; nothing's changed." His tone was curt and resigned, cynical even. I felt like he wanted me to join him in resignation and respond with something like, "You're right. There really is no hope for you. Sorry. Be sure to pay your bill on the way out."

Instead I said firmly, "No, you're wrong. We have made progress and you're not the same man who walked in the door six months ago. I'm very sad, very disappointed that you acted out. It affects me because I care about you; if I didn't, I wouldn't be meeting with you. Tell me about what happened." I then questioned Ed about the feelings and circumstances leading up to his failure. I let myself feel the deep ache in this man's soul as he finally softened and shared his intense loneliness, his hunger for godly brothers, and a longing for the father he never had. We wept together.

I ended the session this way: "Ed, I don't think you really want me to call you on the carpet or preach you a sermon about how terrible you are for what you did. You admitted what you did was wrong. You even admitted that you deeply love God despite the rage you feel at times. I think what you really want today is for me to remind you of what I see in you—a strong man honestly pursuing God, a man who sometimes fails but who does indeed have a strong, repentant heart. If you didn't, you wouldn't be here. I challenge you to be that man I see who loves God, who hates suffering the loneliness and grieving the loss of a father who should've been in your life but wasn't. And despite your struggles and failures, even more so because you don't give up, I care about you and I know our Father cares about you. Even when you or I might give up, He never does. I challenge you to be as strong as you are and seek Him in the midst of your sexual struggles."

Evidently, the people Ed had previously shared his struggle with hadn't handled it too well. They were shocked or repulsed, afraid or insecure because of their own struggles. Consequently, Ed felt justified in keeping his struggle a secret. However, his desire to know God won out and he decided counseling would be a safer option: he would pay someone to provide authentic relationship with him.

Sadly enough, this is often what counseling, especially Christian counseling, amounts to—a safe place for real people to struggle. That's not to say that counseling doesn't serve important roles, emotionally, psychologically, and spiritually. But counseling is often abused by the Church as a kind of "fix-it" station where problems can be resolved and joy restored. This in itself reflects the very problem—the Christian community's unwillingness to allow pilgrims to struggle and to suffer with them. So often church is the place we feel most reluctant to be real about what's going on in our lives when it should be the place we feel most welcome.

How do we overcome this? How can the Church become that place where honest struggle is not only permitted but *encouraged* as an opportunity to know the Father better? First, we need to take the risk to seek out trustworthy people who love the Lord within the church body. Break the silence of secrecy about what goes on in your heart and give others the chance to love you. Second, reconsider your own perception and participation in your community. Respond to others out of grace and a willingness to share what they both suffer and rejoice. Provide them with the freedom to be real with you.

The biblical undergirding for this is certainly implicit in Christ's command to love. But it is also explicit in the letter of James: "Make this your common practice: Confess your sins to each other and pray for each other so that you can live together whole and healed. The prayer of a person living right with God is something powerful to be reckoned with" (5:16, MESSAGE). What James calls confession I interpret as an honest sharing of our struggles and failures. Richard J. Foster, in his *Celebration of Discipline*, interprets it similarly:

Confession is so difficult a Discipline for us partly because we view the believing community as a fellowship of saints before we see it as a fellowship of sinners. We come to feel that everyone else has advanced so far into holiness that we are isolated and alone in our sin. We could not bear to reveal our failures and shortcomings to others. . . . Therefore we hide ourselves from one another and live in veiled lies and hypocrisy.

But if we know that the people of God are first a fellowship of sinners we are freed to hear the unconditional call of God's love and to confess our need openly before our brothers and sisters. We know we are not alone in our sin. The fear and pride which cling to us like barnacles cling to others also. We are sinners together. In acts of mutual confession we release the power that heals. Our humanity is no longer denied but transformed.[1]

3. What's presently your biggest obstacle to authentically sharing your struggles with others?
4. How would you want someone to respond after having heard you share your hardest struggle? Why? How would such a response make a difference?
5. What are the dangers of confessing to others? The benefits? Do you believe it's presently worth the risk with certain people in your life or not? Why, or why not?

A CHALLENGE TO SEEK GOD: BORROWING FAITH

My dear friends, if you know people who have wandered off from God's truth, don't write them off. Go after them. Get them back and you will have rescued precious lives from destruction and prevented an epidemic of wandering away from God. (James 5:19-20, MESSAGE)

As you can see from my description of Ed, as well as James's and Foster's words about confession, allowing ourselves and others to struggle authentically is closely connected to the second major trait of godly community: the challenge to seek the Father amidst that very struggle. If we are only encouraging one another to share honestly for its own sake, then we amount to no more than a navel-gazing, self-absorbed community of complainers and whiners. Somewhere in the midst of our struggle we long to see God, to know that He's present and sovereign even though we can't necessarily feel His presence or see His hand the way we'd like to. We want others to remind us of what He's done for us in the past, what He's doing for them (and us) presently, what our hope for the future is. Battered and bruised, we want to lean on the faith of others for just a few steps of the journey. We borrow that faith and let it nourish our own.

And sometimes they're battered and bruised as well and we lean on each other. Or sometimes we can be there to remind others of the Father's presence and goodness in all our lives. We remind them of a bigger picture, a bigger plan than the momentary suffering, discomfort, or doubt. We enter into and share their fears and longings. We pray for them when they can't pray for themselves. We weep, laugh, sing, eat, shop, or play with them. We share our being with them and give them Christ, not a facade of perfection when we're so far from it ourselves.

This often means letting others see our own struggles and doubts, and hopefully, our passionate obedience in the midst of it. We let the seams of life show, how we don't have it all together, that we get mad sometimes, say things we regret, overspend our budgets, and still pray, hope, and love anyway.

I recently heard a pastor preach a sermon on sexuality. His thesis was that sexuality is a sacrament (not a Christian sacrament like baptism or communion), a holy connection between a man and woman within marriage that illuminates a glorious picture of God, Heaven, and His longing for us. He illustrated the violation of this sacrament with an anecdote about a friend's bachelor party in their younger days. An unattractive woman had been hired to strip at the all-male party as a joke. When she came to the party and began to perform, the men felt saddened; the joke backfired. Even the prankster who had hired the woman in the first place couldn't laugh. They had violated their sexuality and the woman's, and they knew it and were saddened by it. The pastor told the story at what I consider great personal risk and vulnerability. He showed his own weakness for a higher purpose; in his weakness all of us in the congregation saw God's strength, His purpose for holy sexual expression, not the cheap degradation that we often pursue.

Self-disclosure is important because it points back to the Father's purposes, His goodness in the past, His mercy and grace in all its odd forms and extensions. This is often what we find in the Psalms, the full range of struggles—doubt, fear, anger, joy, danger—and testimony to God's goodness and deliverance. This is what we see David doing in Psalm 51, sharing openly the depths of his guilt, sorrow, and desire to change in order to testify to God's mercy and goodness.

> 6. Describe a time in your life when someone has pointed you back to God. How did borrowing his or her faith affect your own faith journey?

THE LOVE OF CHRIST: GIVING SELFLESSLY

Finally, a rich, godly community will be permeated with the love of Jesus, a sense of concern, caring, thoughtfulness, and boldness that we see demonstrated continually in our Savior's life. This love, in fact, is the fuel energizing the first two traits. Without love, allowing room for struggle does become self-absorption; without love, seeking God can lead to cynicism and despair. The love of Christ reveals itself in our willingness to bear the burdens of others, to care when they don't, to remind them of who they are and who God is. Loving with the love of Christ means living out of faith with our hearts tuned to hope. Such a love provides us with cold drinks of Heaven in the midst of our parched, fallen world.

Thanks to Christ's sacrificial example, God's grace, and the indwelling of the Holy Spirit, there's a quality in our earthly relationships that reflects the complete fulfillment we will have someday with the Father. This intimacy whets our appetites for the ultimate love we will experience in Heaven.

When we connect with a friend or family member and cry together over a shared struggle or celebrate God's presence together in a prayer or song, we taste a divine morsel. The rich connection of souls takes us out of ourselves and into the struggles and passionate life of another human being. We don't feel so alone or so strange or so isolated in our own efforts to live. Instead of competing with or fearing one another we feel a side-by-sideness as we journey together.

When passionately relating to God out of repentant hearts becomes the priority of ourselves and others, we experience community as God intends it. Such empowering love shows that God uses relationships and community to remind us of His presence and to mirror His love to others. Since we can't see our Father physically as He is, we see Him in the eyes and actions of friends and loved ones, and they see Him in us. The Apostle John explains it this way:

> Dear friends, let us love one another, for love comes from God. Everyone who loves has been born of God and knows God. Whoever does not love does not know God, because God is love. This is how God showed his love among us: He sent his one and only Son into the world that we might live through him. This is love: not that we loved God, but that he loved us and sent his Son as an atoning sacrifice for our sins. Dear friends, since God so loved us, we also ought to love one another. No one has ever seen God; but if we love one another, God lives in us and his love is made complete in us. (1 John 4:7-12, NIV)

As John points out, loving relationships are only possible with God as our source. Sanctification, the process of holy change that God produces throughout our lives, occurs as we wrestle with loving others because we love God. And as we've seen in the other chapters, this means interrupting the habit of always considering our needs and desires more important than others'. True community develops as a byproduct of this process, spurring us on to a hope and a calling bigger than our emotional needs.

ACCOUNTABILITY

In many ways, if you've experienced the three characteristics of true community, then it's not necessary to define and discuss accountability. It naturally exists. However, since this is not often the case, let's examine what it means to hold each other accountable.

Steve trudged into his friend Dan's office and closed the door. They chatted for a few moments and Dan could tell that Steve was nervous about something.

Finally, Dan asked, "Are you okay? Have something on your mind you want to talk about?"

"I was wondering when you were going to ask. I've been struggling hard this week; in fact, yesterday I really failed. I promised I'd tell you when it happened, so I'm telling you." Steve almost seemed matter-of-fact about it, rather than sorrowful as Dan had experienced him after their first discussion.

"What would you like me to do about it?" Dan asked sincerely. "I'm not a police officer, you know. I care for you and pray for you, and yes, I'm disappointed. But how can I help you or love you when you treat me like your parole officer?"

Steve bowed his head, speechless. Dan continued, "Steve, being accountable to me doesn't mean I can read your mind. Yes, I will ask how you're doing, but I expect you to share your heart with me whether or not I ask the right question."

"Does this mean you don't want to meet with me?" Steve finally asked.

"No, not at all. But if I'm nothing more than a policeman

giving you a speeding ticket, then I can't help you, and frankly, I don't want to be used that way. True accountability is about relationship, in this case, about brotherhood."

Accountability often takes on negative connotations. We have the Big Brother mentality of someone looming over our shoulder, policing our every move, waiting to pounce on our failures. This may be followed by a lecture, a minisermon, scripture recitation, or pat answers. Either that, or accountability goes to the other extreme, where we recite our week's top-ten sin list to our friends, listen to them tell us theirs, and then both say, "That's okay. See you next week." In either case, true accountability is being violated.

Many of us avoid accountability because we've experienced it as so legalistic and severe that there's no context of community, caring, or Christ's love. Or, we've emphasized the relational atmosphere of total acceptance and indifference so much that little, if any, encouragement or change results. True accountability, on the other hand, combines both elements—a call to holiness and a reminder of Christ's love—to create a relational environment of discipline and grace.

Regarding discipline, there must be some reminder of what God's call to repentant living is. Such a call to holiness reminds us of who we are, redeemed image-bearers (men and women with repentant hearts), and who God is (our loving Father continually accepting us through grace). When the people to whom we're supposedly accountable simply say, "No big deal; I've done worse," they're not loving us at all. They should be challenging us to be broken by our sinfulness, sharing with us a deep and abiding sorrow, loving us gracefully, and calling us to a deeper repentance.

Unfortunately, however, holding others accountable has come to mean "beating up" on them. While accountability always has consequences, it does not mean simply delivering a lecture or quoting a verse. Primarily, true accountability includes relational consequences. Not that you quit being their friend or excommunicate them from the church if they keep on sinning (these are last resorts), but rather that you suffer their sin with them. You are deeply saddened by their hateful words toward their spouse, you feel the shame of their secret sin, you ache with their hunger for restoration. And you share these consequences with them. In fact, many times you may feel what they should feel more deeply, calling them to a place where they become eager for God's Spirit to work in their hearts.

I have a friend who has developed a fail-proof accountability diet. Let's say he wants to lose ten pounds. He simply sets a reasonable time limit, say three months, and if he hasn't lost the ten pounds by then, he has to pay me a thousand dollars. So far it's worked perfectly; my friend would so hate paying me the thousand dollars that he loses the weight.

Sometimes concrete consequences are appropriate means in an accountability relationship. But they must be a means to an end, to the ultimate goal of being more like Christ, loving Him more and knowing the Father's goodness far beyond what you could imagine otherwise. That's why accountability fails so often: the consequences, if there are any, dead-end to legalism or self-righteousness. We end up avoiding sin just so we can tell our friend that we had a "good" week, or we lie and slip back into secretive isolation where it feels like no one can handle our sinful struggles. We need accountability that points out the heinousness of our sin and yet loves us with the excruciatingly real love of Christ.

The purpose of accountability is not so much to change our behavior as to remind us of the change we're experiencing in our hearts, to remind us that what has taken place between us and God in the past has not been erased or invalidated but will continue into eternity. The Apostle Paul describes it this way:

> You've all been to the stadium and seen the athletes race. Everyone runs; one wins. Run to win. All good athletes train hard. They do it for a gold medal that tarnishes and fades. You're after one that's gold eternally.
>
> I don't know about you, but I'm running hard for the

finish line. I'm giving it everything I've got. (1 Corinthians 9:24-25, MESSAGE)

The author of Hebrews follows up his recitation of the
"Christian Hall of Fame"—Old Testament heroes and heroines
of the faith—in chapter 11 with this:

> Do you see what this means—all these pioneers who
> blazed the way, all these veterans cheering us on? It
> means we'd better get on with it. Strip down, start run-
> ning—and never quit! No extra spiritual fat, no parasitic
> sins. Keep your eyes on *Jesus*, who both began and fin-
> ished this race we're in. Study how he did it. Because he
> never lost sight of where he was headed—that exhilarat-
> ing finish in and with God—he could put up with any-
> thing along the way: cross, shame, whatever. And now
> he's *there*, in the place of honor, right alongside God.
> When you find yourselves flagging in your faith, go over
> that story again, item by item, that long litany of hostility
> he plowed through. *That* will shoot adrenaline into your
> souls! (Hebrews 12:1-3, MESSAGE)

The authors' choice of athletic metaphors in both passages is
doubly deliberate: it not only motivates us with the intense fervor of the most passionate coach, but it also illuminates how we
can help each other in the race. Accountability is, in essence,
running alongside others—shouting encouragement, offering
water, sometimes nudging them along in our stride.

When I first became friends with my wife-to-be, Dotti offered
me both accountability and encouragement. During a particularly intense struggle with depression and doubt, I began to withdraw a bit from Dotti, under the "spiritual" justification that I
complained too much to her by sharing my struggles. One afternoon I came home and found a note from her on my apartment
door that deeply encouraged me by reminding me of the fierce,
uncomfortable emotions of the psalmist and how he continually

cries out to God despite his pain. Her note closed with, "Please do not be afraid to share the tough days as well as the good ones. Or else how will I be able to tell you about mine? How will we know to lift each other to our Father?" Her concern and her gentle reminder to a higher calling manifested through our relationship allowed me to see that I was withholding myself out of fear and self-protection, not out of concern for her. I felt the freedom and the responsibility to share genuinely, even the negative emotional junk I usually tried to hide.

Accountability is about relationships with other people, not about being better or worse, spiritually superior or inferior. There is certainly a place to consider spiritual maturity (or immaturity) in choosing people to trust and share your life with. However, the best accountability relationships are built on mutual concern and love for one another, and the mutual direction of repentant hearts set on loving the Father, set on the path leading to Christlikeness, set on the path for Home.

7. Why do you suppose it's easier to exercise the extremes of accountability—either too legalistic or too lax—rather than the relationship of accountability?
8. How do you feel as you read Paul's description of the faith "race"—energized, discouraged, frustrated, hopeful? What do you connect your feelings to?
9. Describe the kind of accountability you long for. What steps can you take to develop that kind of relationship?

JOURNALING THE JOURNEY

From My Journal

I went walking tonight around the neighborhood with Scott, and we started reflecting on our friendship over the past three years, how we met, what we first thought of each other, all that's hap-

pened since then, our respective daughters being born. I love the way he puts things. For instance, Scott says that he believes the angels rejoice when people, even two, get together to know God better. When he and I go walking in the evening and talk about our lives, we don't feel so alone, so lonely as men. Scott even said that he feels more energized and motivated to love his wife well, to be a better father, not because of me or any example I set (that's for sure!) but because of what I point him toward and what he points me toward.

Our walk made me reflect on my other relationships. When I meet with Scott, Stacey, John, or other friends, or when I talk at a heart level with Dotti, I come away hungrier. I want more of two things: first, I want more of them, more of that wonderful sense of connection that can occur between two hearts set on the same goal, following the same calling; and second, I want to live a more godly life. It's odd, the way the two go hand in hand. Because of the way they reveal God to me, I want to know more of Him, to be more of Him to other people in their lives. I think this is why we are fundamentally relational beings and why we're also fundamentally alone. God designed the tension between the two to remind us of Him, of what we were created for, that kind of childlike intimacy that Adam and Eve once had in the garden.

For Your Journal

Who makes up your spiritual community? What relational risks would you like to take to strengthen your relationships, to develop accountability? Whom do you miss who has shown you glimpses of Christ and has moved away or died? Who would you like to reach out to? Make a list of practical ways you can love others and exercise your repentant heart this week.

8

INTIMACY
WITH THE FATHER

—

On a popular television sitcom, George, the klutzy side-kick, bounces like a pinball from one backfiring experience to another. He tries to ask a woman out for a date and ends up making a fool of himself; he goes for a job interview and unknowingly insults his prospective boss. In one episode George finally tires of his misfortunes and decides to change his relational style: since he usually follows his first impulse with disastrous results, George decides that from then on, he'll say or do the exact opposite of what he typically does. The consequences are wonderful. Although he becomes blunt, direct, and open about his true feelings and motives, he discovers that people are attracted to such candor. He gets the date with the beautiful model, he gets hired at the job of his dreams.

While this television character's motives are purely selfish, I believe his strategy often reflects the way many of us approach repentance. We think to ourselves, *Well, what I really want is to feel loved and appreciated by my family, but instead of acting so needy, I'll become aloof.* Or, *Instead of saying what I really think, which often comes across as harshly honest, I'll remain quiet.* Thus, we change our behaviors but our heart motives remain the same, fixated on self-protection or manipulative gratification. But if this is our approach to living out of a repentant heart, then we're really no further than when we started.

Ironically, George's approach to personal change contains an element of truth. While there is no formula for living out our repentance—acting the exact opposite of how you typically do is *not* a good approach—often we do need to risk outside of our usual comfort zones. Such risk taking will help us face the fears, inconvenience, and discomfort that often come with moving into other people's lives because of a greater love, a greater goal, than self-protection or self-gratification.

This will naturally look different on different individuals. For many of us, becoming more disciplined in the way we spend our time, especially in prayer and reading of Scripture, will flow out of our repentant heart. For others, however, who have been legalistically motivated to have a regular quiet time out of a rote sense of guilt-induced obligation, going for a walk, reading a child a story, or meeting a friend will reflect the changes of our heart. Understand that I am not advocating that repentance means we should give up prayer, Bible study, and spiritual disciplines. On the contrary, a truly repentant heart will be drawn to them magnetically by the hungry obedience of the will in accord with the leading of the Spirit. But for some of us who have turned our Christian lives into management projects, reducible to a formula or spiritual recipe that "guarantees" success, genuine change will likely include backing away from old legalistic methods and reapproaching what it means to know and seek the Father. In these areas, repentance may indeed mean shelving our seven-point Bible study manuals for a season and simply spending time alone with God, in conversation with Him, journaling about our relationship with Him, talking to a trusted Friend.

The implications of this are indeed broad, and that can be dangerous. For instance, a teetotaler who used to condemn anyone who even looked at a beer bottle should not suddenly be getting drunk down at the local bar every night. Even though this indeed might reflect a change of heart, the freedom of Christ is being abused. On the other hand, living out of a repentant heart does not mean putting blinders on to the culture around us and focusing solely on the Christian subculture. Many Christians—new Christians especially—believe that repentance for them means giving up every vestige of their former lives, and indeed it may. However, simply switching from MTV to Christian music videos, putting a Christian symbol on our car, and hanging out only with other Christians is not what sanctification is all about.

In considering the personal, individual choices of lifestyle, behavior, and everyday living, two essential guidelines for living out of a repentant heart emerge: (1) the freedom we have in Christ and (2) the call to righteousness we have in Christ. Let's consider these individually.

THE FREEDOM OF CHRIST

Christ has set us free to live a free life. So take your stand! Never again let anyone put a harness of slavery on you.... It is absolutely clear that God has called you to a free life. Just make sure that you don't use this freedom as an excuse to do whatever you want to do and destroy your freedom. Rather, use your freedom to serve one another in love; that's how freedom grows. (Galatians 5:1,13-14, MESSAGE)

A repentant heart is a free heart. When we experience the sorrow of our bondage to sin, the way we consistently attempt to make our lives work for us apart from God and the joy of grace, the way our Father lovingly receives and forgives us despite our stubborn rebelliousness, *then we experience freedom.* The sorrow of our sinful inclinations keeps us humbled and incredibly grateful. The joyful embrace of grace thus becomes a place of rest, liberty to love, and intimacy with the One who knows us better than anyone.

Living out of this freedom means feeling what you feel as

you feel it. That's not to say that we shouldn't use self-discipline, restraint, and other-centeredness to channel the expression of our emotions. But we should feel the freedom to pretend about nothing, to be honest with our Lord and God and cry out to Him in joy and pain and rage and relief. Being aware of such freedom because of the relationship we have with the Father often allows us to let go of old habits and motivations. What might this look like?

Michelle replaced the phone on the cradle and smiled to herself.

"Who was that?" Brian yelled from the next room. "Another telemarketer?"

"Not exactly," she replied. She walked into the living room where her husband was helping their children with their coats. "It was Cathy from the hostess committee at church begging me to head the Spring Missions Banquet."

"Wow, is that coming up already? That's always a lot of work for all of you on the hostess committee." Brian tried not to be immediately negative about what he knew was a worthwhile cause.

"Well, I told her I can't lead the committee this year. I'll be a part and help out with the desserts, but I don't have to be in charge of the whole thing. I don't have to be in charge of everything for it to happen, and that feels good. I still feel a little guilty, a little afraid of what Cathy and the others might think of me, but that's okay."

Brian kissed his wife and held her coat as she slipped into it.

"What's the big surprise?" Josh, their youngest, asked. "Will you tell us where we're going now?"

Brian winked at Michelle before responding, "Well, your mom had this great idea for all of us to go . . . ice-skating!" The children screamed with glee and Michelle felt the Father's love shining through her to her family.

Living out of the freedom we have in Christ requires us to be more flexible, more spontaneous, more attuned to those around us, and more loving. It also means we become less self-conscious, less controlling, less self-absorbed. While we may still struggle with old feelings and the inclinations to make life work like we used to, we choose to act on faith, aware of the tender flame of the Father's love burning within us, the source of our identity and purpose.

1. How would you define the freedom we have in Christ?
2. How have you lived it out in the past? How might you live it out differently now?
3. Make a list of freedoms that you desire to live out based on your repentant heart.

THE CALL TO RIGHTEOUSNESS

> My counsel is this: Live freely, animated and motivated by God's Spirit. Then you won't feed the compulsions of selfishness. For there is a root of sinful self-interest in us that is at odds with a free spirit, just as the free spirit is incompatible with selfishness. These two ways of life are antithetical, so that you cannot live at times one way and at times another way according to how you feel on any given day. Why don't you choose to be led by the Spirit and so escape the erratic compulsions of a law-dominated existence? (Galatians 5:16-17, MESSAGE)

Notice the way Paul's instruction to live righteously goes hand in hand with living out our freedom in Christ. This call to vertical living makes it clear that we are not to abuse the freedom we have under grace (see Romans 6) by sinning according to our old natures. Rather, we experience the freedom of the Spirit, and this fuels our desire to live more godly lives, courageously suffering through the pain of circumstances, unruly emotions, and the damage done to us by others. Even more importantly, the freedom we have in Christ allows us to face the sorrow of how we think only of ourselves, hurt others, and grieve the Father. Such holy conviction motivates us to make new choices, to love others, to give of ourselves, to seek out the quiet places alone with our Abba.

When this kind of change is allowed to grow within us, we no longer have to be on a quest to "find ourselves," our purpose and identity, because we have been adopted as our Abba's children. We know who we are only because we're more intent on knowing God.

Brennan Manning describes the process this way: "The meaning of our lives emerges in the surrender of ourselves to an adventure of becoming who we are not yet."[1]

Righteous living is not necessarily easy; we will still suffer, struggle, fail, and doubt at times. But we will not be attempting to live righteously on our own, for appearances' sake like the Pharisees. Paradoxically, righteous living does become easier out of the passionate relationship we have with our Father.

When my daughter started taking her first steps, she would look to me (or my wife) for approval. When we smiled and clapped, she would then take off again, eager to go farther, to stay on her feet just a little longer. The same is true for us and our Father. We desperately long for His embrace and touch, to be ushered up onto His lap, hugged and loved. And in Heaven we will have just that. However, for now we must keep walking, seeing His smile and pleasure reflected in others, in His surprises, in His grace-gift to us, Jesus.

Steve felt the itch within his soul, the desperate hunger for relief from his loneliness, fear, and the disappointment in his marriage. It was five o'clock, his work day ended, and he had a choice to make. He picked up the phone.

"Dan, this is Steve. Would you pray for me? I'm about to leave work and I don't feel like going straight home. Yeah, I am scared and lonely. . . . It's been a hard week. Well, I remembered what you said last week about the Father's love, about the freedom I have because of who He is and who He made me to be. I want so much more than a quick flip through a magazine. And that means suffering my temptations for what I really long for, to know our Father. Yeah, I know. Thanks."

Steve hung up the receiver and felt the internal churning subside just a little. He picked up the phone and dialed another number.

"Hi, honey, it's me. Yes, I'm just about to leave. I just thought I'd call and see how you're doing, how your day's been. Good. Really? That's great." Steve felt a stronger love pulling at his heart, the love of His Father shining through the voice of his wife. "I'll see you in about twenty minutes. I love you."

As he drove home down the freeway, Steve thought about why he hadn't gone to the adult bookstore. He wasn't sure why, couldn't quite put words to it. All he knew was that something bigger was going on inside, something that had to do with him and God, with his hunger to know His Father, to be with Him at home for eternity. He wanted to love his wife and father his kids with this same kind of love. He knew he'd still struggle, that his battle wasn't necessarily over. But he knew that a greater war was indeed over; his faith was growing, stretching his heart to a deeper calling of love and the freedom of obedience.

The call to righteous living, our obedience in faith to the voice of the Spirit within us and to God's Word, becomes most effective when activated by the awareness of our freedom. Again, let me stress that it still might not be any easier; on the contrary, life might feel harder, your struggles deeper, and your faith more challenged. When we honestly face the reality of this world, it drives us to either sink deeper into mediocrity, "just getting by" as we passively wait or manipulatively manage, or to seek God. A repentant heart faces the full force of circumstances, painful emotions, and the existential questions of faith ("Where are you, Lord? What should I do? Why am I here? Why did this happen to me?") because it honestly wants to know the Father's Truth. God is more than powerful enough and good enough to handle our doubts, fears, frustrations, and failures. He is always running down the path, arms outstretched, eager to hold us, reassure us of His love, remind us of our true worth as His children.

4. What signs do you see that Steve is beginning to choose righteousness out of a longing for the Father, not out of shame or legalistic duty?
5. Can you imagine yourself making the kind of free, righteous choices Steve is beginning to make? Why?

INTIMACY WITH THE FATHER

Bottom line, beneath this awareness of freedom and the call to righteousness, repentance comes back to relationship with God. While we often pay this phrase lip service, I believe we rarely seek to live it out, to risk, ask, and act with God. Recall from our discussion about the prodigal son in chapter 1 that we defined repentance as "coming to our senses." Such a turning pulls us back to the Father whom we may fear, rightfully so, but whom we also long to know intimately. The prodigal at least knew his father well enough to know that even in his most furious, punitive mood, his dad would still let him work as a servant with decent shelter and fresh food. But again, how far this falls from the grace bestowed to him. His father actively grieved the separation between them, ached, longed for his child to be in his arms again. His child's return to him, the wonderful restoration of relationship, required—no, demanded—celebration. This picture reminds us that God's longing for relationship surpasses His holy wrath at how we spit in His face with our rebellious disobedience. Why else would He sacrifice His Son, abandon Him to a despicable death of nail-pierced flesh and splintering wood? He loves us. It's that utterly simple.

In his book *The Return of the Prodigal Son*, Henri Nouwen compares the parable from Luke 15 with Rembrandt's masterful painting and shares how the two have intersected in his life. What attracted him most from his very first encounter with the portrait was the father's hands, his tender expression as his son kneels before him. One hand is rugged and firm, a very masculine hand. The other is soft and smooth, almost delicate, the hand of a mother. The father embraces his wayward child with compassion, a depth of understanding that goes unspoken, a tenderness that breaks into the lonely, parched heart with a deep river of forgiveness, love, and hope. The father embraces his child with strength, with a resting place of grace. Nouwen writes, "Rembrandt portrays the father as the man who has transcended the ways of his children. His own loneliness and anger may have been there, but they have been transformed by suffering and tears. His loneliness has become endless solitude, his anger boundless gratitude."[2]

The loving father's transformation here serves as a powerful model of who we are becoming as we live out of repentant hearts. We do indeed view our loneliness and sufferings as opportunities for solitude, aloneness with God. In an address in Toronto, Nouwen once described solitude as being alone, pausing in silence, so that you can hear the Father's voice call you beloved.

How often in our DayTimer-packed days and hectic race from home to office to church and back again, do we make time, create time to be truly alone with the Father? Repentance requires time. It is not only an ongoing process requiring the time of our lives, but it requires time for aloneness, for vertical reflection (not self-absorbed internalization), for spiritual disciplines. If we are truly hungry for change, for returning to our Father's embrace, for staying on the heavenly path that we are asked to walk, then we will find the time because it matters most to us.

I believe the spiritual disciplines—solitude, prayer, Bible study, fasting, etc.—are so easily misused because we schedule them too easily and reduce them from being facilitators of solitude and mystery and worship to being formulas with "guarantees." Like any aspect of the Christian life, they can be abused through the extremes—relying on them to make change happen in themselves or ignoring them altogether because they require sacrifice. They are simply vehicles, reminders of God, paths that when followed consistently lead us to the vacant places of our heart so that we hear God's voice, feel His embrace.

It's like trying to squeeze through a huge crowd to get to the other side in order to reach your Beloved, the truest desire of your heart. You must push past all the demands and responsibilities in your life, the demands of people, your wants and whims, emotions, commitments ranging from extremely important to trivial—from making time for spouses and other essential relationships to dropping off desserts for the church picnic—and keep moving toward the Father. Spiritual disciplines are simply ways to move past the throng that would swallow you up in itself and clear a smooth, tranquil spot where you can visit with your Abba.

When I was a boy growing up in Tennessee, the church I attended had a traditional baptistery behind the pulpit. On the wall behind the small pool, a local artist had painted a mural, a heavenly mural in my estimation. It was a lovely, pastoral scene with a river rendered in blues and sea green flowing through a countryside. Purple mountains peaked over the horizon. A willow tree arched across one lush, emerald bank.

It was a glimpse of Heaven for me and still is. It is a place I return to again and again to meet with my Father. I work to get there with a hunger I cannot describe. And of course, I fail. I get busy, and tired, and lazy. I find all kinds of excuses for not meeting God there through prayer and Bible study, discipline and service. But I work to overcome them because of a desire that is greater than the temporal whims that often overtake me. Again as Nouwen describes it, practicing the spiritual disciplines allows us to create a space where God can surprise us.

Jesus describes Himself as the example and the bridge to surprising intimacy with the Father:

"I am the Real Vine and my Father is the Farmer. He cuts off every branch of me that doesn't bear grapes. And every branch that is grape-bearing he prunes back so it will bear even more. You are already pruned back by the message I have spoken.

"Live in me. Make your home in me just as I do in you. In the same way that a branch can't bear grapes by itself but only by being joined to the vine, you can't bear fruit unless you are joined with me.

"I am the Vine, you are the branches. When you're joined with me and I with you, the relation intimate and organic, the harvest is sure to be abundant. . . .

"I've loved you the way my Father has loved me. Make yourselves at home in my love. If you keep my command, you'll remain intimately at home in my love. That's what I've done—kept my Father's commands and made myself at home in his love." (John 15:1-5,9-10, MESSAGE)

Notice the way freedom ("You are already pruned back by the message I have spoken") and righteous obedience ("Live in me") work in unison to produce spiritual transformation and fruit of the Spirit. We "make ourselves at home" in Christ's love, in who we truly are, in our true worth as men and women bought with the steepest price imaginable, by first accepting the gift of grace and then choosing to live it out. "If you keep my command, you'll remain intimately at home in my love." If we obey God and seek Him, exercising faith, activating the hope of a repentant heart, then we taste the sweet embrace of our Father's love.

Joanne looked out across the vista of mountains, pine trees, and blue skies. The sun fell warm across her face, and she leaned back on the giant boulder where she sat. The wind whispered. Wild flowers in pinks and purples and yellows waved to her from the fields.

There was a stillness inside her that she often resisted. It meant facing loneliness, fear, uncertainty. However, she had come up to this spot to yield to it. To meet God on the other side of it.

Her friend Mary had suggested that she go away for a spiritual retreat, a time of aloneness between her and God. While it sounded good at first, Joanne knew that it would be one of the hardest things for her to do. No distractions. No television, CDs, shopping trips, business projects, fellowship dinners, or singles excursions. No motivational speakers, self-help books, or romance novels. Just herself, her Bible, and a God bigger and more beautiful than the splendor of His creation before her.

It wasn't easy, but it felt right and true. It felt good to respond to a deeper yearning, a more heartfelt hunger than she usually allowed herself to face. And despite the loneliness and its discomfort, something was happening inside that she couldn't even begin to describe. "Be still, cease striving and know that I am God," she paraphrased from Psalm 46:10. It felt like she was learning to do just that.

6. When have you experienced intimacy with God? How did it happen?
7. What would it be like for you to be alone with your Father this week? How has He surprised you in the past with His goodness, concern, mercy, or love?

LIVING WITH THE LONGING
OF A REPENTANT HEART

As I hope you have seen throughout this book, repentance is an ongoing process of grief over our self-centeredness and joy over the Father's loving gift of grace. Repentance requires a commitment to the Father, not to self-improvement, that transcends all the suffering, the weight of all our uncomfortable emotions, and the circumstances of a fallen world. As we have seen from the examples of Christ and Paul, in both their lives and descriptions, a truly repentant heart longs for the joy set before us, the embrace of the Father, the intimacy of relationship with our Creator so much that these temporarily sufferings can be endured (Romans 8:18).

Eugene Peterson states, "[Repentance] is always and everywhere the first word in the Christian life."[3] We keep moving, stumbling, failing, but we go on, not because we're confident of our own abilities, but because we trust in the Father to sustain us.

The prophet Ezekiel speaks for the Lord to the people of Israel, "I will give you a new heart and put a new spirit within you; and I will remove the heart of stone from your flesh and give you a heart of flesh. And I will put My Spirit within you and cause you to walk in My statutes, and you will be careful to observe My ordinances" (36:26-27). The Apostle Paul affirmed, "For I am confident of this very thing, that He who began a good work in you will perfect it until the day of Christ Jesus" (Philippians 1:6). As C. S. Lewis so aptly points out in the conclusion to the quote (the dentist analogy) I cited in the introduction, we ourselves are the only thing that can stop God from perfecting us:

> God's demand for perfection need not discourage you in the least in your present attempts to be good, or even in your present failures. Each time you fall He will pick you up again. And He knows perfectly well that your own efforts are never going to bring you anywhere near perfection. On the other hand, you must realize from the outset that the goal toward which He is beginning to guide you is absolute perfection; and no power in the whole universe, except you yourself, can prevent Him from taking you to that goal. That is what you are in for. And it is very important to realize that.[4]

Do you want to change? Do you want to know the Father? No matter what you've done, even since you've accepted Christ, His grace is ever before you. Have you lied to others to protect yourself, cheated on your tax return, fed a sexual addiction, withdrawn from your spouse, had an affair, worshiped all the false idols this world offers? His arms are wide and warm. Are you aware of the tight, clenched selfishness within your being? Feel His embrace, His hands on your shoulder; give this same blessing to others as you can, and continue on the journey. Know that you are forgiven, that you are changed. Know your true worth, your true calling and destination. Trust that He is faithful in His love, goodness, and power even when nothing or no one around you seems to indicate it. Exercise this hope, this faith; take risks. Continue on the journey.

JOURNALING THE JOURNEY

From My Journal

It is late at night and I cannot sleep because I can't quit think-ing about what I want to say in this last chapter. What do I know about intimacy with the Father? What do I have to say about repentance for that matter?

When I proposed this book, I was in the midst of a counsel-ing internship in which I met with fifteen individuals and one group composed of eleven of those individuals. It was a remark-able experience that showed me the best and worst in people and how they relate to God. But what I observed that made me want to write this book was that people were changing despite themselves. God was using me despite myself as well.

Let me explain. I counseled a woman for eight months and each week felt like a repeat of the week before; she'd come in, complain about what a bad hand she'd been dealt by God, and share that week's crisis that only confirmed her case. And she had lived a horrible, hard life filled with childhood abuse, a hus-band who didn't seem to love her, children who demanded her attention, and a church that set an impossible standard of the perfect Christian woman.

As a fairly inexperienced counselor, I wasn't quite sure what to do. Each week I tried a different strategy, always trying to point her to view God differently, what I considered more accu-rately, but she always out-talked me, and I sat patiently trying to get a word in edgewise. Once I even told her that she didn't need me; I threatened to leave my office door unlocked and let her talk to my chair the next week. She wasn't fazed.

The last few weeks we were together a different woman came in. No, she hadn't had a complete make-over. She looked the same and was even prepared to complain about her week. However, in our final session she stopped herself after the first ten minutes. "I know you may not believe it, but I'm different than I was when I first came in eight months ago. God feels different to me because of you."

I sat there incredulously. Of all my students and clients, she was the one with whom I thought I had failed the most. While she had seen numerous counselors before (and been diagnosed borderline) and, after all, I was still a novice, I still felt I had let her down. After my shock wore off, I asked, "Wendy, what do you mean? I've been afraid I haven't helped you at all."

"Oh, but you have. You've been so patient with me. You've listened to every word I've said. Even though I drive you crazy because I complain so much, you still listen. You make me think that maybe God's willing to listen as well. You make me believe that He might even care."

I was moved. God seemed incredibly tangible in this woman sitting across from me, who indeed had annoyed me considerably. My point has nothing to do with my sanctity, counseling model, or therapeutic skill. It has everything to do with my inability, with Wendy's willingness to look for God even when I didn't think she cared to look for Him. I felt a strange kind of intimacy with my Father at that moment, a kind of confidence I used to feel when I was a child and my bike would break down. "Dad will know how to fix this," I'd say to myself, and he usually would. Now as an independent, capable, competent adult, I rarely rely on my Father. But God so often reminds me of His presence through my lack of control, my inability, even ineptness. He doesn't care whether or not I can change a flat tire, pass the state counseling licensure exam, or memorize the New Testament. He cares about me, about this despicably fickle heart that's beating His breath through my body even as I type this. He calls me son. He calls all of us sons and daughters.

Writing this book has been one of the most challenging endeavors of my life, certainly of my career. A friend recently told me that he couldn't wait to read it and I visibly winced. "What's wrong?" he asked.

"I worry about being seen, about what people will think about what I have to say. Writing this kind of book is more vulnerable than writing fiction. With a novel I can always fall back on 'it's only a story, something I made up,' but with a book on repentance, either I'm connected to it or I'm not." And either way feels incredibly vulnerable—if my heart's in it, then I'm seen by hundreds of people; if I'm detached from it, then I'm also seen, perhaps as just someone wasting words about one of the most personal and powerfully profound topics.

Repentance is about making consistent decisions to seek a goal bigger than self. Repentance is about relationship.

I live with this picture in front of me on my desk: the photograph of a man holding a boy in his lap. The father (presumably) is sitting on pavement or on a curb; he wears a jacket from a thrift store, a white button-down shirt, jeans, and red high-top sneakers. The boy in his lap has his eyes closed and is almost smiling; maybe he's sleeping. The boy wears a grey sweatshirt and jeans that are cuffed above his ankles and bare feet. The man has his arm around the boy's shoulder and his head bent into the boy's face as if he is kissing his forehead or simply pressing his face into the boy's. Sometimes I glance up at it and tears spring from some deep well. Sometimes I smile to myself when I walk by and look at it. I think of my daughter and the ways I experience God through her and to her. The photograph encapsulates so much for me, so much longing and grief, so much hope and yearning. It seems right for me to look at it each day to be reminded. Maybe it reminds me of who I am and who I want to be. It reminds me of my Abba. I will keep it before me. I pray that you keep it before you as well.

For Your Journal

What do you feel as you finish this book? Where do your mind and heart go? What do you want to happen in your life? What will you do differently tomorrow toward that goal?

How will you cultivate intimacy with the Father? How will you find that clear space where He longs to call you His beloved?

What pictures come to mind that remind you of your Father's presence in your repentant heart?

NOTES

—

Introduction—Do You Want to Change?
1. C. S. Lewis, *Mere Christianity* (New York: Macmillan, 1960), page 171.

Chapter One—Why Do I Do What I Don't Want to Do?
1. Dan B. Allender, *The Wounded Heart* (Colorado Springs, CO: NavPress, 1991), page 202.

Chapter Two—Temptations
1. Hannah Whitehall Smith, *The Christian's Secret of a Happy Life* (Waco, TX: Word, 1984), page 182.
2. M. Basil Pennington, *A Place Apart* (New York: Doubleday, 1983), page 180.
3. Thomas à Kempis, *The Imitation of Christ* (Grand Rapids, MI: Zondervan, 1983), page 185.

Chapter Three—Addictions
1. Gerald May, *Addiction and Grace* (San Francisco: HarperCollins, 1988), page 3.
2. May, pages 19-20.
3. Oswald Chambers, *Christian Disciplines*, vol. 2 (New York: Dodd, Mead, and Co., 1935), page 288.

Chapter Four—The Feelings of Repentance
1. Oswald Chambers, *Christian Disciplines*, vol. 2 (New York: Dodd, Mead, and Co., 1935), page 262.
2. Dan B. Allender and Tremper Longman III, *Cry of the Soul* (Colorado Springs, CO: NavPress, 1994), page 33.

3. William Nevins, as quoted in *12,000 Religious Quotations*, ed. Frank S. Mead (Grand Rapids, MI: Baker, 1988), page 377.
4. Eugene Peterson, "Introduction to 1 and 2 Peter," *The Message: The New Testament in Contemporary English* (Colorado Springs, CO: NavPress, 1993), page 486.

Chapter Five—Penance Versus Repentance
1. Frederick Buechner, *Wishful Thinking* (New York: Harper and Row, 1973), page 15.
2. *The Book of Common Prayer* (New York: Seabury Press, 1979), page 352.

Chapter Six—Exercising a Repentant Heart
1. Martin Luther, as quoted in *12,000 Religious Quotations*, ed. Frank S. Mead (Grand Rapids, MI: Baker, 1988), page 377.
2. Eugene Peterson, *A Long Obedience in the Same Direction* (Downers Grove, IL: InterVarsity, 1980), pages 165-166.
3. Frederick Buechner, *Wishful Thinking* (New York: Harper and Row, 1973), page 29.
4. Buechner, page 79.

Chapter Seven—Community and Accountability
1. Richard J. Foster, *Celebration of Discipline* (San Francisco: Harper and Row, 1978), page 127.

Chapter Eight—Intimacy with the Father
1. Brennan Manning, *Abba's Child* (Colorado Springs, CO: NavPress, 1994), page 157.
2. Henri Nouwen, *The Return of the Prodigal Son* (New York: Doubleday, 1992), page 139.
3. Eugene Peterson, *A Long Obedience in the Same Direction* (Downers Grove, IL: InterVarsity, 1980), page 25.
4. C. S. Lewis, *Mere Christianity* (New York: Macmillan, 1960), page 172.

AUTHOR

—

Dudley J. Delffs is a writer and an English instructor at Metropolitan State College of Denver and Colorado Christian University. He holds degrees in English from the University of Tennessee and in biblical counseling from Colorado Christian University, where he also interned under the supervision of Dr. Larry Crabb. He lives in Littleton, Colorado, with his wife, Dotti, and daughter, Mary Elise.

His previous works include the novel *Forgiving August* (Piñon Press, 1993) and study guides for the THINKING THROUGH DISCIPLESHIP series (NavPress, 1993).